Marshall McLuhan
by DOUGLAS COUPLAND

With an Introduction by
John Ralston Saul
SERIES EDITOR

EXTRAORDINARY
CANADIANS

PENGUIN
an imprint of Penguin Canada

Published by the Penguin Group
Penguin Group (Canada)
90 Eglinton Avenue East, Suite 700, Toronto, Ontario, Canada M4P 2Y3

Penguin Group (USA) Inc., 375 Hudson Street, New York, New York 10014, U.S.A.
Penguin Books Ltd, 80 Strand, London WC2R 0RL, England
Penguin Ireland, 25 St Stephen's Green, Dublin 2, Ireland (a division of Penguin Books Ltd)
Penguin Group (Australia), 707 Collins Street, Melbourne, Victoria 3008, Australia
(a division of Pearson Australia Group Pty Ltd)
Penguin Books India Pvt Ltd, 11 Community Centre, Panchsheel Park,
New Delhi – 110 017, India
Penguin Group (NZ), 67 Apollo Drive, Rosedale, Auckland 0632, New Zealand
(a division of Pearson New Zealand Ltd)
Penguin Books (South Africa) (Pty) Ltd, 24 Sturdee Avenue, Rosebank,
Johannesburg 2196, South Africa

Penguin Books Ltd, Registered Offices: 80 Strand, London WC2R 0RL, England

First published in Penguin hardcover by Penguin Canada, 2009

Published in this edition, 2013

Printed in the United States of America

LIBRARY AND ARCHIVES CANADA CATALOGUING IN PUBLICATION

Coupland, Douglas
Marshall McLuhan / by Douglas Coupland ; with an introduction by John Ralston Saul.

(Extraordinary Canadians)
Includes bibliographical references.

ISBN 978-0-14-317090-7

1. McLuhan, Marshall, 1911-1980. 2. Mass media specialists—Canada—Biography.
I. Title. II. Series: Extraordinary Canadians

P92.5.M3C69 2013   302.23092   C2013-900589-7

Visit the Penguin Canada website at www.penguin.ca

Special and corporate bulk purchase rates available; please see
www.penguin.ca/corporatesales or call 1-800-810-3104, ext. 2477.

Coupland's profile of McLuhan, although quirky and off-beat, takes pride of place among the already stellar offerings in Penguin's Extraordinary Canadians series.... Coupland's seems to capture the essential McLuhan; keen, astute, discerning, a prophet with well-earned honour in his own land."   —*London Free Press*

"Coupland has given us the McLuhan of the Internet era."
                                              —*The Vancouver Sun*

Praise for the Extraordinary Canadians series

"These books are not definitive biography; rather, they are opportunities to deepen the relationship between Canadians of the past and Canadians of the present. May this dialogue continue, so that today's biographers themselves will be the subject of the next wave of writers." —*The Globe and Mail*

"The concise books are a vivid, 'character-driven patchwork' of modern Canadian history made relevant to modern readers. In other words, no dry academic tomes allowed.... What's compelling about the Extraordinary Canadians series is that it draws you back to some of the original oeuvres—to

Praise for *Marshall McLuhan*

"It's the best of the Extraordinary Canadians series thus far, both for its readability and for its meditations on writing biography in the 21st century. There is also a near-perfect fit between biographer and subject...." —*Toronto Star*

"This is an affectionate, wry portrait that provides a perfect introduction to one of the most influential and misunderstood thinkers of recent times." —*The New Republic*

"Insightful.... What emerges as indisputable is McLuhan's place in Canadian and world intellectual history.... Coupland's considerable achievement is making one understand both the momentousness of McLuhan's intellectual achievement and the quirkiness of the Canadian crucible that nurtured and gave sustenance to it. Bravo."
—*The Gazette* (Montreal)

"Coupland's biography is consistently beautifully written."
—*Winnipeg Free Press*

"Douglas Coupland is a perfect fit to compose a brisk, stylish mini-biography of the legendary Marshall McLuhan....

John Ralston Saul

How do civilizations imagine themselves? One way is for each of us to look at ourselves through our society's most remarkable figures. I'm not talking about hero worship or political iconography. That is a danger to be avoided at all costs. And yet people in every country do keep on going back to the most important people in their past.

This series of Extraordinary Canadians brings together rebels, reformers, martyrs, writers, painters, thinkers, political leaders. Why? What is it that makes them relevant to us so long after their deaths?

For one thing, their contributions are there before us, like the building blocks of our society. More important than that are their convictions and drive, their sense of what is right and wrong, their willingness to risk all, whether it be their lives, their reputations, or simply being wrong in public. Their ideas, their triumphs and failures, all of these somehow constitute a mirror of our society. We look at these people, all dead, and discover what we have been, but also what we can be. A mirror is an instrument for measuring ourselves. What we see can be both a warning and an encouragement.

These eighteen biographies of twenty key Canadians are centred on the meaning of each of their lives. Each of them is very different, but these are not randomly chosen great figures. Together they produce a grand sweep of the creation of modern Canada, from our first steps as a democracy in 1848 to our questioning of modernity late in the twentieth century.

All of them except one were highly visible on the cutting edge of their day while still in their twenties, thirties, and forties. They were young, driven, curious. An astonishing level of fresh energy surrounded them and still does. We in the twenty-first century talk endlessly of youth, but power today is often controlled by people who fear the sort of risks and innovations embraced by everyone in this series. A number of them were dead—hanged, infected on a battle-field, broken by their exertions—well before middle age. Others hung on into old age, often profoundly dissatisfied with themselves.

Each one of these people has changed you. In some cases you know this already. In others you will discover how through these portraits. They changed the way the world hears music, thinks of war, communicates. They changed how each of us sees what surrounds us, how minorities are treated, how we think of immigrants, how we look after each other, how we imagine ourselves through what are now our stories.

You will notice that many of them were people of the word. Not just the writers. Why? Because civilizations are built around many themes, but they require a shared public language. So Laurier, Bethune, Douglas, Riel, LaFontaine, McClung, Trudeau, Lévesque, Big Bear, even Carr and Gould, were masters of the power of language. Beaverbrook was one of the most powerful newspaper publishers of his day. Countries need action and laws and courage. But civilization is not a collection of prime ministers. Words, words, words—it is around these that civilizations create and imagine themselves.

The authors I have chosen for each subject are not the obvious experts. They are imaginative, questioning minds from among our leading writers and activists. They have, each one of them, a powerful connection to their subject. And in their own lives, each is engaged in building what Canada is now becoming.

That is why a documentary is being filmed around each subject. Images are yet another way to get at each subject and to understand their effect on us.

The one continuous, essential voice of biography since 1961 has been the *Dictionary of Canadian Biography*. But there has not been a project of book-length biographies such as Extraordinary Canadians in a hundred years, not since the Makers of Canada series. And yet every generation understands the past differently, and so sees in the mirror of these remarkable figures somewhat different lessons. As history rolls on, some truths remain the same while others are revealed in a new and unexpected way.

What strikes me again and again is just how dramatically ethical decisions figured in these people's lives. They form the backbone of history and memory. Some of them, Big Bear, for example, or Dumont, or even Lucy Maud Montgomery, thought of themselves as failures by the end of their lives. But the ethical cord that was strung taut through their work has now carried them on to a new meaning and even greater strength, long after their deaths.

Each of these stories is a revelation of the tough choices unusual people must make to find their way. And each of us as readers will find in the desperation of the Chinese revolution, the search for truth in fiction, the political and military dramas, different meanings that strike a personal chord. At first it is that personal emotive link to such figures which draws us in. Then we find they are a key that opens the whole society of their time to us. Then we realize that in that 150-year period many of them knew each other, were friends, opposed each other. Finally, when all these stories are put together, you will see that a whole new debate has been created around Canadian civilization and the shape of our continuous experiment.

At the heart of that experiment lies a continuous revolutionary approach toward communication. It is somehow spatial, not linear; it has been postmodern from the beginning. It was, and still is, there in First Nations philosophy. It took on a more or less Westernized form with Harold Innis, and from Innis sprouted Marshall McLuhan, who would find the words and language and gestures for people around the world to imagine themselves communicating in a different way. And remarkably, all of this was done long before most of the technology to make it possible existed. Out of what I would call the Toronto School—including, beyond Innis and McLuhan, people such as Glenn Gould and Northrop Frye—came a universal revolution in how we could think together.

Douglas Coupland is not just a wonderful novelist and artist. He is in and of himself the contemporary expression of McLuhan's theories, the natural child of McLuhanism, and therefore the perfect biographer for the man who broke the shackles of linear communications.

... return

shaman larch mull
shaman march lull
shaman charm lull
shaman mall lurch
llama harms lunch
llama marsh lunch
llama marls hunch
llamas harm lunch
alarm halls munch
alarm shall munch
alarm malls hunch
alarm small hunch
alarms hall munch
alarms mall hunch
haunch mall marls
launch harm malls
launch harm small
launch harms mall
launch marsh mall
larch humans mall
larch human malls
larch human small
ranch mullah lams
ranch mullah slam
ranch mullah alms
clan mullah harms
clan mullah marsh
clans mullah harm
larch hall man sum
larch ham mall sun
larch ash man mull
larch has man mull

larch all man hums
larch all man mush
larch alls man hum
clash hall man rum
clash hall ran mum
clash ham mall urn
clash ham mall run
clash ham ram null
clash ham arm null
clash ham ran mull
clash rah man mull
clash mall ran hum
clash man ram hull
clash man arm hull
march ash man lull
march has man lull
march all man lush
charm ash man lull
charm has man lull
charm all man lush
chasm ham ran lull
chasm rah man lull
chasm all man hurl
ranch lash all mum
ranch ham all slum
ranch all lams hum
ranch all slam hum
ranch all alms hum
char hall man slum
char lash man mull
char ham lams null
char ham slam null

char ham alms null
char ham man lulls
char mash man lull
char sham man lull
char hams man lull
char mall man lush
char lams man hull
char slam man hull
char alms man hull
arch hall man slum
arch lash man mull
arch ham lams null
arch ham slam null
arch ham alms null
arch ham man lulls
arch mash man lull
arch sham man lull
arch hams man lull
arch mall man lush
arch lams man hull
arch slam man hull
arch alms man hull
crash ham man lull
cash harm man lull
cash mall man hurl
call hah snarl mum
call ham snarl hum
call ham man hurls
call harm man lush
call mash man hurl
call sham man hurl
call hams man hurl

call marls man huh
calls ham man hurl
calm hah mall runs
calm hah mall urns
calm hah malls urn
calm hah malls run
calm hah small urn
calm hah small run
calm hah mars null
calm hah rams null
calm hah arms null
calm hah ran mulls
calm shah mall urn
calm shah mall run
calm shah ram null
calm shah arm null
calm shah ran mull
calm hash mall urn
calm hash mall run
calm hash ram null
calm hash arm null
calm hash ran mull
calm hall ham runs
calm hall ham urns
calm hall harm sun
calm hall mash urn
calm hall mash run
calm hall sham urn
calm hall sham run
calm hall hams urn
calm hall hams run
calm hall man rush

calm hall ram shun
calm hall arm shun
calm hall ran hums
calm hall ran mush
calm halls ham urn
calm halls ham run
calm halls ran hum
calm shall ham urn
calm shall ham run
calm shall ran hum
calm lash man hurl
calm ham rash null
calm ham ran hulls
calm harm ash null
calm harm has null
calm harm all shun
calm mash rah null
calm mash ran hull
calm sham rah null
calm sham ran hull
calm hams rah null
calm hams ran hull
calm rah mall shun
calm rah man hulls
calm rash man hull
calm mall ran hush
calm malls ran huh
calm small ran huh
clam hah mall runs
clam hah mall urns
clam hah malls urn
clam hah malls run

clam hah small urn
clam hah small run
clam hah mars null
clam hah rams null
clam hah arms null
clam hah ran mulls
clam shah mall urn
clam shah mall run
clam shah ram null
clam shah arm null
clam shah ran mull
clam hash mall urn
clam hash mall run
clam hash ram null
clam hash arm null
clam hash ran mull
clam hall ham runs
clam hall ham urns
clam hall harm nus
clam hall harm sun
clam hall mash urn
clam hall mash run
clam hall sham urn
clam hall sham run
clam hall hams urn
clam hall hams run
clam hall man rush
clam hall ram shun
clam hall arm shun
clam hall ran hums
clam hall ran mush
clam halls ham urn

The name of a man is a numbing blow from which he never recovers.

M.M.

Marshall McLuhan's online-generated Porn Star name[1]
... Pud Bendover

Marshall McLuhan's online-generated Pimp name
... Slick Tight

Marshall McLuhan's online-generated Ho name
... Skanka

Marshall McLuhan's online-generated Prison Bitch name
... Piglet

Marshall McLuhan's online-generated Emo name
... Abandoned by God

Marshall McLuhan's online-generated Drag name
... Vanilla Thunderstorm

Marshall McLuhan's online-generated Pirate name
... Jake the Well Tanned

Marshall McLuhan's online-generated Mexican Wrestler name
... Ratón Fuerte

Marshall McLuhan's online-generated Goth name
... Lord Fragrant Desiccated Corpse

Marshall McLuhan's online-generated RPG name
... Incomparable Brilliant Katana

Marshall McLuhan's online-generated Outlaw Biker name
... Ol' Boozy Beefy Junkie MC

---

[1] Names selected by placing the name Marshall McLuhan into commonly available internet name generators.

The next medium, whatever it is—it may be the extension of consciousness—will include television as its content, not as its environment, and will transform television into an art form. A computer as a research and communication instrument could enhance retrieval, obsolesce mass library organization, retrieve the individual's encyclopedic function and flip it into a private line to speedily tailored data of a saleable kind.

M.M.
1962

The Seer

The year is 1980 and it is spring. A man is lying on a couch in a cool, dark office in a quiet, suburban Tudor home. He is almost seventy years old. He is left-handed. He is hetero-sexual. He is in the city of Toronto, Ontario. He is staring at the ceiling. He is white. He is wearing a sweater over a button-down collared shirt. His name is Marshall. It is hard to know what is going through Marshall's mind because something has happened to him. He can no longer speak. He can no longer read. He can no longer write. This has been going on for half a year now, since he had his stroke. Oddly, he can perfectly understand what people are saying when they speak to him—but he can't generate words him-self. And while he can also listen to the radio or watch TV, and understand what people there are saying, once the voices stop, the words in his head stop, too. What has happened to the voice inside his head—is it dead? For that matter, is it even possible for one's inner voice to die? And if so, what would that silencing sound like? What can the sound of no voices *be*?

Marshall sees a bee trapped inside the room, batting itself on the windowpane. *Tappa-tappa-bzzzt, tappa-tappa bzzzt* ... He stands up and rescues the bee, and as he does so, he says, *boy-oh-boy-oh-boy*—the two words he has been left with after the previous autumn's gross insult to his brain, the words he says when he agrees with something. The outside air smells of lawn clippings and pollen. In the distance a dog barks. Marshall turns around and looks at his room: books stacked higgledy-piggledy on most available flat surfaces, an almost cartoonishly don-like office. It is killing Marshall that he looks at his books and can't even generate the word *book* himself. He knows that these books and papers represent his life. And then, suddenly, something happens. A radio in another room in the house is playing a Protestant hymn and, although he has been a fervent Catholic for over forty-two years, he begins to belt out the hymn's lyrics. But the hymn ends, and so does Marshall's singing. He is returned to his world of sound effects, and he again surveys his books, many of which are books he wrote, so he knows them by their shape and colour but not their titles. Life is cruel and life is humbling. Marshall knows that he was once considered one of the best talkers in the world. He knows that he once had ideas that changed the way people looked at the world and at life, but again, he has been reduced to sound effects. But Marshall also knows that he once punned like a god. He knows that he once ruled a kingdom of anagrams and double entendres, and that his life's core themes revolved around how we communicate from person to person, from generation to generation, and from one century to the next. He knows he'd seen the future of the future. He knows he'd become world renowned and world reviled, and now he can't even say a proper goodbye and good luck to a goddamn *bee*.

Timesickness

Part of writing a biography involves asking why we should care about the subject. In 1989 a terrific biography of Herbert Marshall McLuhan was published, and an equally terrific biography was published in 1997. During these years Marshall was largely a boutique intellect for a small group of people whose thought patterns mapped closely onto his own—academics and people working in the outer fringes of media, professionally and academically.

But somewhere around 2003 the texture of daily life inside Western media-driven societies began to morph, and quickly, to the point where, a half-decade later, it's now obvious to people who were around in the twentieth century that time not only seems to be moving more quickly, but is beginning to feel *funny*, too. There's no more tolerance for waiting of any sort. We want all the facts and we want them *now*. To go without email for forty-eight hours can trigger a meltdown. You can't slow down, even once, ever, without becoming irrelevant. Music has become more important because music is a constant. School reunions are beside the point because we already know what our old classmates have done. Children often spend more time in dreamland and cyberspace than in real life. Time is speeding up even faster.

And then the economy collapsed in a weird way that felt like a hard-to-describe mix of Google, *The New York Times*'s website, pop-up ads for Russian pornography websites, and psychic radiation emitted by all those people you see standing by the Loblaws produce section at 6:15 on a weeknight, phoning home to see if spinach is a good idea. All this information and more has overtly, osmotically, or perhaps inadvertently damaged a collective sense of time that has been working well enough since the Industrial Revolution and the rise of the middle classes. This "timesickness" is probably what killed the economy, and God only knows what it's up to next. Everywhere we look, people are making online links—to conspiracy, porn, and gossip sites; to medical data sites and genetics sites; to baseball sites and sites for Fiestaware collectors; to sites where they can access free movies and free TV, arrange hookups with old flames or taunt old enemies—and time has begun to erase the twentieth-century way of structuring one's day and locating one's sense of community. People are now doing their deepest thinking and making their most emotionally charged connections with people around the planet at all times of the day. Geography has become irrelevant. Our online phantom world has become the new *us*. We create complex webs of information and people who support us, and yet they are so fleeting, so tenuous. Time speeds up and then it begins to shrink. Years pass by in minutes. Life becomes that strange experience in which you're zooming along a freeway and suddenly realize that you haven't paid any attention to driving for the last fifteen minutes, yet you're still alive and didn't crash. The voice inside your head has become a different voice. It used to be "you." Now your voice is that of a perpetual nomad drifting along a melting landscape, living day to day, expecting everything and nothing.

And this is why Marshall McLuhan is important, more so now than ever, because he saw this coming a long way off, and he saw the reasons for it. Those reasons were so new and so offbeat and came from such a wide array of sources that the man was ridiculed as a fraud or a clown or a hoax. But now that we've damaged time and our inner voices, we have to look at McLuhan and see what else he was saying, and maybe we'll find out what's coming next, because the one thing we can all agree on is that the future has never happened so quickly to so many people in such an extreme way, and we really need a voice to guide us. Marshall identified the illness and worked toward finding ways of dealing with it.

> To bring order into this jangled sphere man must find its centre.
> M.M.

Science Meets Fiction

In 1962 McLuhan wrote,

> Instead of tending towards a vast Alexandrian library the world has become a computer, an electronic brain, exactly as an infantile piece of science fiction. And as our senses have gone outside us, Big Brother goes inside. So, unless aware of this dynamic, we shall at once move into a phase of panic terrors, exactly befitting a small world of tribal drums, total interdependence, and superimposed co-existence.

In one stroke, Marshall anticipated—four decades in advance—the internet, although there was far more than this one stroke. The man was fifty-one when he published those words, a Canadian professor of Renaissance rhetoric, a man who perpetually stated his loathing and contempt for most of the electronic age, yet a man who perversely and ironically is considered its biggest cheerleader.

At the same time, drawing on his own arcane studies of early English prosody and rhetoric, and a vast array of sources ancient and modern, some of astonishing obscurity, Marshall warned us that without a key to understanding this new cyberspace universe, it held a terrifying capacity for rumour, disinformation, and surveillance—terrors he saw that would be built on the inability of a newly global and essentially oral culture to shade, test, and nuance. And they are terrors of which we are only beginning to grow aware.

"Terror," he went on to say,

> is the normal state of any oral society, for in it everything affects everything all the time ... In our long striving to recover for the Western world a unity of sensibility and of thought and feeling we have no more been prepared to accept the tribal consequences of such unity than we were ready for the fragmentation of the human psyche by print culture.

Obvious and Yet Not

Okay. The thing about a genius idea is that, the moment someone hears it, they say, "Well *that's* obvious."

When hit with a genius idea, people also tend to say, "Well, if I sat down in a chair and really thought about it, I

17

could have had that genius idea, too." But they didn't—and even if they'd wanted to, it could never have happened. For a person to have a genius idea, millions of biographical factors need to be in place, and if even one of those factors is missing, well, there goes the genius idea. We never know what those millions of factors are going to be, or which person they're going to be happening to. Take Bill Gates as an example: more or less the richest man on earth, and friends with the other richest men on earth. He is also either friends with and/or employs the most measurably scientifically intelligent people on earth. So here is Bill Gates and all those people going off to sweat lodge retreats and Davos forums, all the while trying to figure out what happens next. What happens next is that they *didn't* think of Google. They *didn't* think of social networking. And they *didn't* think of the iPhone. Ideas don't happen where they're supposed to. Marshall's career is proof of this.

Environments are invisible. Their ground rules, pervasive structure, and overall patterns elude easy perception.
M.M.

McLuhan: The Brand

Inasmuch as history remembers people, it also needs to peg them. McLuhan is pegged for two ideas that went on to become clichés: "the medium is the message" and "the global village." He did much more, but those words are his brand, so to speak.

"The medium is the message" means that the ostensible content of all electronic media is insignificant; it is the medium *itself* that has the greater impact on the environment, a fact bolstered by the now medically undeniable fact that the technologies we use every day begin, after a while, to alter the way our brains work, and hence the way we experience our world. Forget the ostensible content, say, of a television program. All that matters is that you're watching the TV itself, at the expense of some other technology—probably books or the internet. Those media we *do* choose to spend our time with continually modify the way we emphasize our senses—seeing versus hearing versus touching—on a scale so large and spanning so many centuries that it took at least a decade after Marshall's death for him to be proven right, with the triumph of the internet.

Marshall's other cliché, "the global village," is a way of paraphrasing the fact that electronic technologies are an extension of the human central nervous system, and that our planet's collective neural wiring would create a single 24-7 blobby, fuzzy, quasi-sentient metacommunity.

And one must remember that Marshall arrived at these conclusions not by hanging around, say, NASA or IBM, but rather by studying arcane sixteenth-century Reformation pamphleteers, the writings of James Joyce, and Renaissance perspective drawings. He was a master of pattern recognition, the man who bangs a drum so large that it's only beaten once every hundred years.

There is a third idea that needs to be remembered here, too: the man in his cool, quiet office, allowing a bee to escape from his window, had been a superstar. At a certain point in the mid-1960s he stopped being merely a brainy academic from Toronto. He became a massive brand, as famous and synthetic and misunderstood and misquoted as fellow 1960s media construct and artist Andy Warhol. The mass media loved Marshall because his intricate theoretical positions both mystified and flattered them. In the early 1960s there were no media studies courses; Marshall literally invented them. And there was famously—as C.P. Snow's *The Two Cultures* observed—no linking of high culture to pop culture, or of literary and artistic literacy to the scientific and technological, each despising the other. But Marshall saw the world as utterly interlinked and ensured that all forms of culture were grouped together—which is possibly why his ideas have weathered the years since his 1980 death while others have fallen away.

At the start of his fame curve, when Marshall was first
proposing ways to understand new media, he was often nas-
tily ridiculed by the establishment either for what he seemed
to be saying, or for saying it in ways that made people feel
like they needed a translator.[2] And by the last ten years of his
life, his fame had dwindled and he had become, in some
ways, his own worst enemy, defending his theories by over-
selling them and trying to make them clearer by rendering
them so terse and aphoristic that they seemed to be an
almost secret language.

As a result, these days, most people who know McLuhan's
name have only a fuzzy idea of what he said and did—and
these fuzzy ideas themselves are based on second, third,

---

[2] "There is afoot a mindless orgy of trend-catching anti-literacy, best typified by the appalling popularity of the jargon-laden, hyped-up, and profoundly ahistorical works of McLuhan, designed to flatter just about all the
prejudices of a TV generation in which functional illiteracy is already well
advanced." This is a quote from Peter Green, a Yale professor, author of
Classical Bearings: Interpreting Ancient History and Culture (London:
Thames & Hudson, 1989). However, I originally found this quote on an
internet site without attribution. When I typed five words of it into
Google Book Search's beta version, the source was provided and most of
the book was made available to me—instantaneously and free of cost. The
book had been scanned by Google, and then character recognition programs made it a fully ASCII-searchable document. Seven million books,
mostly out of print (including Peter Green's), had been scanned by Google
at the time of this search.

fourth, and nth degrees of handedness. His highly idiosyn-cratic way of thinking and writing is easily parodied. But the thing about parody is that it tells you a style is so potent that it can be, well, *parodied*. Parody is a backhanded compli-ment from people who think they're actually trashing their intended victim.

In a way, McLuhan's ideas become like a song we all know the tune of but not the full lyrics, and so we read into him whatever comes to mind. Forget poor-players and strutting; twenty-first-century life is karaoke—a never-ending attempt to maintain dignity while a jumble of data uncontrollably blips across a screen.

Tellingly, Marshall's fans tend to be hard core. For them he becomes a personal friend and guide, one who helps decode the karaoke of modern life with a charged intensity. It's this intensity that tells me the man was foremost an artist, one who happened to use ideas and words as others might use paint. And when he spoke in front of classes or in front of baffled AT&T executives or in front of tripping Bay Area freaks, he was also enacting performance art of the highest calibre.

That's roughly how we have thought of him. But what might he think of us? I think he'd be horrified to have been proven so right on so many levels, and he'd also be glad like crazy to be living in eternity and not in our worldly future. He hated the modern world and he hated technology, but that never prevented him from being obsessively *interested* in the world it produced and fanatic about trying to understand it. Marshall was crotchety and obtuse, and probably lived too entirely inside his head to be fully likeable (though I'm sure likeability was something he couldn't have cared less about). But boy-oh-boy-*boy*, did he string together words in a way that now seems like dense, fabulous poetry! And he saw the world as a book created by God, and believed that there is nothing in it that cannot be understood—and that we fail to try understanding it at our peril.

For tribal man space itself is the enemy because it is charged with voodoo menace. For such a man the beautiful is that which suggests the indestructible or the invulnerable. Just as, for the time-frayed the womb-like security of the limousine is beautiful because it promises pneumatic bliss.

M.M.

Surviving in the McLuhan Era

Around the same time I was researching this book, I was writing a novel called *Generation A*, a quasi-sequel to my book published in 1991, *Generation X*. When that first book came out, I was placed into a McLuhan-ish situation in which a creative work involving pattern recognition ended up at the core of an unsightly media frenzy. Marshall's situation was much larger than my own, but there are definite parallels between us. (I'm not going to get into that now. And in no way am I flattering myself.)

Generation X was a *Decameron*-style novel set in the California desert in which young people tried to make sense of an "accelerated culture" by telling each other stories. Implicit in the book was the notion that generations were, by 1991 and thanks to technology, becoming obsolete concepts as we entered an era when each person was becoming a generation unto him- or herself. So years of generation-labelling nonsense ensued, all of which was doomed from the get-go.

Generation A has characters placed in a similar situation, set in the near future in British Columbia's Haida Gwaii, where exiled people are forced to tell stories to make peace within a near-future world in which the "retribalization" of Marshall's global village has been in progress for a decade or so beyond the current moment. One recurring motif in the book is "the Channel Three News team," a metaphor for the interior voice we all use inside our heads to "listen" with while we read. I used them as a metaphor because TV newsreaders are chosen not only for their bland looks but also for their generic yet sonorous voices—voices calculated to appeal to the broadest swath of viewers and listeners by

closely approximating the voices of their own internal narra-
tors. And haven't we all met someone at a party to whom
we've said, "Wow—with your voice you should be on the
radio or TV."[3]

Herewith a quick short story from *Generation A* that also
taps into a strain of apocalyptic thinking that permeated
much of Marshall's later years.

Bartholomew Is Right There at the Dawn of Language

A long time ago a bunch of people were sitting on a
log, looking at a fire, and they were wishing they had
language so that they could talk to each other.
Grunting was becoming a bore, and besides, they had
fire now—they *deserved* language. They'd arrived.

Of course, they didn't think of it that way—they
only had these feelings that went undescribed because
there were no words for them. But within this tribe
there was this one alpha guy in particular who saw
himself as the creative one. He pointed to himself and
said, "Vlakk." He picked up a stick, held it up, stared
at it, scrunched his eyes and then pronounced it
"glink." And everyone there repeated "glink" and
henceforth sticks became known as glinks and Vlakk
was now Vlakk.

---

[3] There's a lovely joke on the back cover of a book published by Twitter:
"When Morgan Freeman reads a book, what voice does he hear in his head?"

Vlakk then pointed at the fire and made up a noise, "unk," and from then on, fire was called unk. And so on. In one night, Vlakk was able to come up with sound effects for dozens of nouns and verbs—gazelles and smallpox and thorns and wife beating—and because it was just one intelligence making up all these new words, the newly evolving language had a sense of cohesiveness to it—it sounded true to itself the way Italian or Japanese does.

However, Vlakk's language creation process made one tribe member—whom he'd named Glog— furious. Glog was thinking, "This is crazy! You can't just go around making up words arbitrarily, based on sound effects!" But of course, Glog didn't have language, so there was no way for him to articulate his anger at the vim with which Vlakk was cooking up new words. And it's not as if Glog had some other, better way of naming things; he was just one of nature's born bitchers and moaners.

Vlakk and Glog and their tribe had many children, most of whom died very young of hideous deaths because it was the distant past and, in general, people didn't last too long. But enough of Vlakk's descendants survived to generate new sound effects that went on to become words.

And of course, Glog's descendants carried his gene for finickiness, and as the new language grew and grew, they continued to protest the arbitrary harum-scarum way Vlakk's descendants gave words to things like "dung beetles" and "ritualized impalement on sharp satay-like bamboo skewers beside anthills." As the language evolved over thousands of years, everyone forgot that words had begun as arbitrary sound effects. Words were now simply words, long divorced from their grunting heritage.

As Vlakk and Glog's culture became more complex, so did its language. Grammar was invented, as was the future tense and gender and verb conjugation and all the things that make learning a new language a royal pain in *la derrière*.

Finally, language entered modern times. If Glog had been king, his far distant grandchild, Bartholomew, would have been his successor. Distant as they were in time, their neocortices were of the same size; Bartholomew was Glog with a good haircut and a fine suit.

Bartholomew was obsessed with new additions to the language. He was particularly incensed by things that caused language to change or evolve. He worked as a copy checker for a large business magazine and spent his lunch hours and weekends writing acid-tipped hate mail to other magazines that incorporated any noun or verb that had entered the language since the dawn of digital culture. *Can't you see how you're diluting the language? Corrupting it! Tell me, what is a jpeg? What a sick and diseased and laughable word it is—it's not even a word! It's a sound effect; a glottal sideshow freak. It's a bastard word—a bearded lady of a word.*

People at the magazine found Bartholomew to be a lovable kook, but they were very careful never to offend him, because, while he wasn't the sort of person to anonymously mail you a dead sparrow inside a cardboard milk box as some form of demented condemnation, there lingered the feeling that he had more subtle, untraceable means of punishing a perceived offender, like maybe he was keeping dossiers on all of them. And every year during the office Christmas party, somebody got drunk and made a mock crime scene investigation of Bartholomew's bookcased folders. Nothing was ever found, but the secretaries in the office would make fun of his cologne. They called it "KGB."

Fortunately, there was Karen from HR, who was able to allow a ray of light into Bartholomew's world. Each morning she dropped off the paper versions of his daily copy work and was able to smile and receive a smile in return from Bartholomew. Karen was the office free spirit. She had a Bettie Page hairdo, a nose ring and black knee socks she'd bought in Tokyo, in Shibuya. Other girls in the office stood outside Bartholomew's office to witness his Karen smile themselves. They knew he was single, and that Carol in the layout department had seen Bartholomew loitering in front of the straight porn section by the newsstand three blocks over from the office.

"Okay," said Karen, "he's no big catch … but he's certainly a big challenge."

Karen tried to come on sexy at first but pulled back, knowing immediately that it was the wrong strategy. This was going to be one tough fish to reel in. So she decided to conquer Bartholomew by email. Short. Sweet. Perky. *Saucy*. Unfortunately, this decision was made right at the tipping point when hand-held devices enslaved the human psyche. Bartholomew was deeply distressed by the collapse of language into chimp-like bafflegab. Oftentimes his co-workers' text messages exceeded his powers of cryptography.

Sl-lip 70 T0ky0 fi135 L8r 70d4y. I\I0, 7l-l3y d0l\l'7 l-l4v3 4 m4(l-lil\l3 5l-l4p3d 1ik3 4 fu(kil\lg ki773l\l 7l-l47 m4k35 5u5l-li.

He took to keeping his office door shut. He grew a beard, and began drinking his own pee from jars. Okay, he didn't grow a beard and drink his own pee from jars, but only because that behaviour would have offended another code that ordered his life—one of sanitation, of bodily purity. But he *was* bunkering himself.

Suffice it to say that, for Bartholomew, the supremacy of PDAs heralded the beginning of the end. Well, maybe not the beginning of the end, because he'd been raised in the Glog family tradition, which was to believe that every moment of life heralded the beginning of the end. Perhaps these newly triumphant PDAs, in some profound way, marked the end of language, which was now imploding on itself in an optical scrapyard of slashes, diacritical marks and pointless numerical intrusions.

One morning Karen was on the subway, going to work, and was in a strange headspace because she was starting to actually fall in love with Bartholomew. Knowing it maybe wasn't the smartest thing to do, she sent Bartholomew a very *lusty* text message.

Wl-l3l\l I g37 70 7l-l3 0ffi(3 2d4y, 137'5 m4k3 p455i0l\l473 10v3 0v3r70p y0ur 14rg3 (0113(7i0l\l 0f 1il\l3d y3110w 13g41 p4d5. Sl-l4rp3l\l yr p3l\l(i1, Big B0y

Bartholomew read this and thought, "Good Lord, language has devolved into a series of strung-together vanity licence plates! I can't be a part of this! I can't!" So when Karen showed up, Bartholomew didn't give her his daily smile. Karen was crushed. She sent a proper email, in perfect English, that said,

Dear Bartholomew,
Earlier today, while I was riding the subway to work, I emailed you a whimsical message. I think it over-stepped the boundaries of "what is correct," but it was meant in jest and I hope you won't think less of me for it. Karen.

The thing is, Bartholomew ignored this email because he was crazy, and the thing about crazy people is that they really *are* crazy. Sometimes you can get quite far with them and you start telling other people,

"So-and-so's not the least bit crazy," and then So-and-so suddenly starts to exhibit his crazy behaviour, at which point you say "Whoa!" and pull back—*People were right: this guy is really nuts.*

Karen's boss, Lydia, saw Karen moping in the lunchroom and said, "Honey, sometimes I think it's almost more polite to be crazy 24-7, because at least you don't get people falling in love with you and making a mess of things."

"But I *love* him."

"Of course you do, sweetie. Pass me the Splenda."

As Karen left the lunchroom, Lydia said to her co-workers, "People always seem to fall in love during that magical space before one person sees the other display their signature crazy behaviour. Poor Karen."

But Karen's heart mended from her break with Bartholomew, and within two years she was engaged to a guy who made sculptures out of cardboard boxes, which he took to the Burning Man festival in the Nevada desert. And life went on. Bartholomew grew older and buggier. People stopped using land-line telephones altogether. Everyone on earth used PDAs, even starving people in starving countries. All languages on earth collapsed and contracted and Bartholomew's endgame scenario was coming true—language was dying. People began to speak the way they texted, and before he was fifty, language was right back to the level of the log and the roaring fire. Bartholomew wondered why he even came to work. Nobody paid any attention to what he did but, as the Glog family motto goes, "Somebody has to maintain standards."

Then one day Karen walked past Bartholomew's office with her by now teenage daughter. His door was open and he was able to hear the two women speak—they both sounded like the Tasmanian devil character from Bugs Bunny cartoons. They turned around and spoke to Bartholomew: *"Booga-booga-ooga-oog?"*

They were asking him if he wanted to go out for lunch, but he understood not a word. He shook his head in incomprehension. The office emptied of staff. Lunch hour ended and nobody came back. Bartholomew thought this was strange. He walked out of his office and walked around his floor. Nobody. *Hmmm.* He went down into the lobby and there was nobody there or in the street, either. He began to walk around the city, but everywhere he looked there was silence. He looked at the TVs that were playing in public spaces: they showed the Channel Three News team's chairs with nobody on them, soccer fields that were empty, traffic cams trained on still roads.

So he walked back to his office and mulled over the situation, which was actually a kind of dream come true for him—no pesky people to further degrade and cheapen the language! But where had everyone gone? He looked at his screen, where the Channel Three News team finally appeared in a box in the centre:

— Hi, you're watching the Channel Three News team. I'm Ed.

— I'm Connie.

— And I'm Frank, and if you're watching this pre-recorded message, it means that the Rapture has finally happened and you've been left behind.

— You know, Connie, people are probably wondering why we're speaking the way we're speaking right now.

— You mean, speaking like people did at the start of the twenty-first century instead of the modern way of speaking based on text messaging?

— That's right, Connie.

— [giggle] It's because the only people watching this prerecorded broadcast are those that never adapted to the new language and were left behind after the Rapture. Language has come a long way since then, Ed.

— And has it!

— In the old days, people worried about words and grammar and rules.

— And it was a horrible mess, wasn't it!

— You said it, Frank. And not the kind of mess you can remove with some club soda and a bit of elbow grease.

— [all chuckle]

— But once people smartened up and began speaking the way they texted and began shrinking language back to its origins in grunts and groans, people became more primal, more elemental ...

— More *real*.

— *That's* the word I was looking for, Connie. More real. More *authentic*.

— and once people became more authentic and more interested in using noises and sounds instead of words to communicate with others, their interior lives changed. The endlessly raging self-centred interior monologues came to an end. A holy peace and dignity fell over their lives. They accidentally became closer to God.

— and now they've gone right into God's lap.

— where we are now, too!

— So farewell from eternity, you sticklers who remain behind.

— Saying good night from the Channel Three News headquarters, I'm Ed.

— I'm Connie.

— and I'm Frank.

— [all] Wishing you a happy forever!

Strange Blood

Marshall's brain was fuelled by fresh blood from the heart through not one but two arteries at the base of his skull, a trait in the mammalian world found mostly in cats and rarely in human beings.[4] As well, people in Marshall's family tended to die of strokes. Marshall himself had countless small strokes during his lifetime—sometimes in front of a classroom of students, where he'd suddenly gap out for a few minutes and then return to the world.

Why mention this medical information? To establish from the get-go that Marshall was not merely different but *very* different, and it wasn't simply in the way he thought; rather, it was because of the biological mechanisms that *made* and *allowed* him to think what he thought. When looking at the millions of factors that need to be in place to create an identity, one obviously can't ignore nurture, but as time passes and our cultural perceptions of personality

---

[4] Although the brain represents only 2 percent of the body weight, it receives 15 percent of the cardiac output, 20 percent of total body oxygen consumption, and 25 percent of total body glucose utilization. The energy consumption needed for the brain to simply survive is 0.1 calories per minute, while this value can be as high as 1.5 calories per minute (100 W) during crossword puzzle solving. Patrick R. Hof and Charles V. Mobbs, eds. *Functional Neurobiology of Aging* (New York: Academic Press, 2000).

become more medicalized, it behooves us to study Marshall's body as well as his family and origins.

Prairie Boy

Marshall's body entered the world on July 20, 1911, in Edmonton, Alberta. If you were trapped on earth in the year 1911, Edmonton was a pretty good place to be. Many people loved it. His parents did—or at least his father did. Marshall's mother was a different case.

A bit of family history: great-grandfather McLuhan's full name was Herbert Marshall McLuhan, McLuhan coming from the original name, McClughan. In 1846 William McClughan, who was both a younger son and an alcohol enthusiast, emigrated to Canada from Ireland's County Down, along with his wife, Mary Edith Bradshaw, and three children. William's 1846 Canadian ocean adventure was atypical for that year in that he and his family arrived in the New World not in one of the potato famine's coffin ships but rather as people with a little bit of money—part of Northern Ireland's Protestant landowning settlement community.

But the money ran out quickly as they settled near Barrie, Ontario. There, William and his three eldest sons worked as loggers. One of these sons, James, Marshall's grandfather, headed farther west into the ungodly tangled mess that is the forests of northwestern Ontario, eventually staking out one hundred acres and becoming a community leader instrumental in establishing the creation of proper communication modes of his era: good roads and telephone services.

In that era, most of Canada west of Quebec was composed of Scottish, English, and Irish mutts who were God-fearing, in theory teetotalling, churchgoing, thrifty, and pretty much all of the clichés one needed to be to endure the gruesome, backbreaking, and lonely job of settling the land. It's almost impossible to imagine how unforgiving the continent was back then. Not only had settlers left behind all forms of comfort and familiarity, but they were settling a land that was largely unmapped, punished by plagues of mosquitoes and black flies, all of which was cyclically refrigerated by appalling winters.

In 1874 Marshall's grandfather James married a lass from Edinburgh, Margaret Grieve. She was a decade younger than James, and highly pious, and together they had nine children. The fourth was Marshall's father: Herbert Ernest McLuhan.

James McLuhan turned seventy in 1907, at a time when that was no commonplace event. But not only did James turn seventy, he chose the occasion to pull up roots and move his family to Mannville, Alberta, then a wild province not two years old. This was a move that could only have inspired both anxiety and awe in those close to him. James was an intelligent and well-respected man. He was fun and gregarious and loved music and dancing and astronomy. He died in 1919 at the age of eighty-two. Family members seem to agree that Marshall must have derived some of his love of being in front of crowds from this man, while James's churchgoing wife, Margaret, is generally seen as the force behind the fierce religious impulses and austerity that marked both Marshall and Herbert. This link also might not be merely one of nurture over nature—both piety and the religious impulse are partially regulated from within the brain's limbic system. Because this relationship is neuro-structural, it is a biologically heritable characteristic.

Marshall's maternal grandparents were nineteenth-century English immigrants from Bristol. His maternal grandfather was Henry Seldon Hall, who settled in Nova Scotia and tried growing hay without luck, then chose to uproot his family to northern Alberta and start afresh there. History is clear about Henry Seldon Hall: he was a mean son of a bitch. He'd read his Bible and he'd beat his farmhands. He was a bully and doled out violent justice to anyone who dared oppose him. One person who saw him for what he was—and who put a good enough face on it until she could escape—was his daughter, Elsie Naomi Hall, born in 1889. She understood that her father was a monster. The moment she was able, at sixteen, she became a teacher at a Baptist elementary school and remained in Nova Scotia while her parents moved to settle in Alberta in 1906. Her schooling to become a teacher was critical to Elsie's future—and to Marshall's—in that while training to teach she learned elocution, a skill not much taught in our century. Students, largely women—or rather, *ladies*—were taught the technique of using the voice and body to powerful effect, bringing alive the great works of literature and poetry. Elsie was a natural. She worked tremendously hard to master it and was, by all accounts, sensationally good at it.

Two years later, for reasons that were never explained, Elsie, now eighteen, moved to Alberta to join her family. It is interesting and telling that the move was never explained. In 1909, people in Anglo Canada simply didn't discuss things. Aunt So-and-So "took to her bed." Uncle So-and-So was "troubled." Reasons for many of life's most pivotal events were neither expected nor given. And so, Elsie's teaching career in Nova Scotia was cut short, and suddenly she was again stuck in the orbit of her nightmare father, albeit in nearby Mannville, where she taught school and lodged in the home of (… drum roll) James Hilliard McLuhan.

James was the father of Herbert, and Herbert was a handsome ladies' man, ten years Elsie's senior, well-spoken and thoroughly popular. Elsie can only have thanked her stars to have a catch like him fall into her lap, while Herbert could say the same thing. They married on December 31, 1909, and within a year the new couple moved to Edmonton, then at the height of a land boom. Herbert opened a business selling real estate, and life for the McLuhans on this optimistic frontier was good. It was into an expansive world that their first child, Herbert Marshall, came on July 21, 1911, followed by his only sibling, Maurice, two years later.

Elsie, the cosmopolitan force in Marshall's life, never lived in a small town again.

When we step into the family, by the act of being born, we do step into a world which is incalculable, into a world which has its own strange laws, into a world which could do without us, into a world we have not made. In other words, when we step into the family we step into a fairy-tale.

G.K. Chesterton

A Bad Match

Elsie and Herbert were a bad match. They had some good moments when they were younger, but as they aged, intractable personality traits doomed their relationship. Elsie was wilful, socially ambitious, in need of some form of creative expression, and, like her father, an emotional yo-yo. Whether by nature or nurture, she had absorbed her father's whip-cracking mood swings and temper. She also disliked men she thought of as weak or unwilling to take a blow. Herbert, ten years older, was cheerful, erudite, and happy to go along with life's flow, and bore none of Elsie's drive or any of her neuroses. But by the end of 1914, with the onset of the First World War, his business collapsed. He enlisted in the army but was soon discharged because of the after-effects of a flu infection, and then, after a short period of uncertainty, he landed a job in Winnipeg in 1915, selling insurance.

The Peg

*Winni*peg.

Glamour and sophistication are relative traits. For Elsie to live in Winnipeg as opposed to Edmonton was a genteel dream, and the city came with a bonus: it was home to the Alice Leone Mitchell School of Expression. There, Elsie could continue her elocution studies. The McLuhans moved into a house on Gertrude Avenue in a nice part of town, and Marshall and Maurice stayed there until they were young men.

Winnipeg was the third largest city in Canada, and when the Panama Canal opened in 1914, both the railways and Winnipeg were hard hit, causing the city to make the wise decision to stabilize its economy through diversification, preparing it better than most to ride out the Depression when it struck. And despite its size (it was smaller than most North American cities) and its asteroid-like location and freakish winters, Winnipeg had become a high cultural beacon in the West, with a ballet, a municipal art gallery, a symphony, and several theatre companies. It was heaven for Elsie, yet her children seemed to prefer the prairies and their enormous skies. In summers the boys stayed with family at a farm south of the city, learning about animals and the land while avoiding a city churning with drifters and polio.

Starting in 1922, when Marshall was eleven, Elsie began a career as a travelling elocutionist, foraying into the country's remote towns and cities to deliver programs of dramatic reading, performing mostly in church halls, and sometimes bringing the boys along with her on the train. These trips further inculcated in young Marshall a highly North

American sense of distance, a sense of the infinite, and, on some subliminal level, a way of appreciating the need for people and information to cross the vastness of the New World. Radio was in its commercial infancy. Phone calls after sunset meant only bad news, most likely death. Communication was largely difficult and expensive—but in this expansive, lonely world, essential. Elocution also taught young Marshall about the Play-Doh aspect of words, their mutability and their ability to morph and change texture on the tongue.

The absence of cosmopolitan diversions in his young life suited Marshall. He was a quiet child, and he and Maurice spent many afternoons with their father, who took an atypical pleasure (for the era) in being with his children as they grew up, possibly to make up for Elsie's increasingly long stints away from Winnipeg.

Herbert and Elsie fought a great deal. More to the point, Elsie fought while Herbert downplayed life's issues, which incensed her. Looking for a man with stronger will, she hectored Herbert and taunted him in ways that could only be sickening to Marshall and Maurice, as they lay upstairs in bed overhearing the cyclical brouhaha. Elsie had her father's cruel streak and was unafraid to show it. Eventually, the boys came to prefer home life when Elsie was away touring.

Whenever she returned, the chaos resumed. Marshall and his mother—both stubborn as rocks—could raise the roof in verbal matches. Elsie, having decided that Herbert was an unwilling opponent, was happy to have, in her son, a worthy sparring partner. One possible long-term result of this could be Marshall's legendarily thick skin. After his trials-by-Elsie, he became emotionally impervious to the opinions of the outside world.

Curiously, Marshall was not a good elementary student and was set to fail grade six when Elsie (not Herbert) came to the rescue and had Marshall put, instead, on academic probation for grade seven. The intervention worked, and Marshall's academic salvation came about when, for whatever reason, he developed a love of English literature. He'd spent eleven years exposed to Elsie's elocution rehearsals, but be it hormones or DNA or a bump on the head that opened a neural dam, it was only then that he became a book-reading machine, obsessed with words and all their aspects: historical, grammatical, and idiosyncratic, as well as (and this is important) the *physical*—the way the mouth forms a word, the way a word becomes art. For Elsie, Marshall's literary conversion was a slice of cake from heaven: not only did she have a sparring buddy in Marshall, but suddenly she now also had an elocution buddy. Almost overnight

Marshall was forced (by and large cheerfully) to remember vast swaths of English literature and poetry—and not merely remember it, but also recite it aloud with *gusto:* crisp enunciation and precise metre and tone, as was demanded by the Alice Leone Mitchell School of Expression. In his later life as an academic and teacher, this skill set would blow people away, especially his future Cambridge classmates, who had been expecting Marshall to be a hinterland yokel but found instead, if not a savant, certainly a classmate to avoid making citation errors in front of.

Not only was Marshall good at recitation, but he was also a born debating machine, able to demolish pretty much anybody in his orbit. This level of skill had to be partly genetic and partly learned. Many of Marshall's ancestors had been great talkers, but as with elocution, after his battles with Elsie, mere schoolteachers or classmates could only have been the easiest of pickings, and he made no bones about correcting anyone who had made an error. One can only imagine the scene in the high school staff room when class lists were being made for the new academic year and Marshall's name came up.

One also wonders what the teenaged Marshall would have been like in person. Chances are he'd be a quiet kid in the corner who didn't say much but who pounced the moment you pronounced a word incorrectly. And chances are he was probably a bit priggish, a trait he kept his entire life. But people do change as they age, and in any event, the teenaged Marshall determined early on that he'd intellectually outgrown his friends and family, especially his father, with whom Marshall had had countless discussions on politics, theology, current events—serious subjects. Marshall liked serious topics. But Herbert, while intelligent, was also uneducated and an autodidact, as was Elsie. Their thinking didn't follow the classical threads taught in universities, and their gambits and onslaughts could come from any direction—great training for anyone who has to wing it conversationally for a living. Marshall's tendency in later life to speak first and find the footnotes later possibly stems from this familial dynamic.

In any event, Marshall intellectually eclipsed his high school teachers long before his graduation. He knew that the fuel his brain craved could only be found in a proper university.

Agreeing to Disagree

In September 1929, one month before the Great Depression began, a painfully skinny (136 pounds; six-foot-one), bookish Marshall, after one misguided please-your-father year studying engineering (little of which rubbed off on

Marshall, who, even decades later, could barely drive a car), entered a four-year B.A. program in the liberal arts at the University of Manitoba—a far wiser choice for a young man obsessed with reading.

Marshall's first two years were pretty much generic courses in English, geology, history, Latin, astronomy, economics, and psychology. And while his thirst for knowledge spanned all subjects, in the end, three dominant threads emerged: English literature, history, and theology.

Religion was central to the culture of the Prairies in the early twentieth century, to the life of the families who lived there, and to their cohesion as a society. Prairie godliness was still largely a quilt of European denominations: Unitarian, Methodist, Baptist, Presbyterian, Lutheran, Ukrainian Orthodox, and Mennonite. It took a God-fearing creed to convert the gift of a pristine New World into one vast food-making engine.

Marshall, raised Methodist, had no problems with Christianity and all of its variants, even though later in life he said he didn't believe in anything until his 1937 conversion to Catholicism. Two Bible-thumping grandmothers had even made him comfortable around apocalyptic modes of evangelism. Meanwhile, Elsie, raised Baptist, became an on-again off-again Christian Scientist who castigated a doubting Methodist Herbert for not coming to church with her and the kids on Sundays. Marshall and his brother were a bit like religious half-castes. Christian Science at the time was definitely not a Bible-thumping denomination but rather a progressive way of being—much concerned with knowledge and debate and inquiry and communication and doubt. It was possibly simply too much work for the easygoing Herbert.

While everybody in the McLuhan family agreed to some extent on Christianity's larger strokes, it was in the details that the squabbling began, and for Marshall and brother Maurice (who went on to become a Presbyterian minister) there arose a need for even bigger strokes—a need for some sort of theological or cosmic master plan. Elsie's Christian Science acknowledged the existence of an all-encompassing view of the world; perhaps Marshall's quest in the succeeding decades stems from that need. A belief in the existence of a master plan largely underpinned Marshall's adult thinking and behaviour, both privately and publicly. His unwillingness to keep specialized realms ghettoized defined him, giving him public fame and academic sorrow.

In and Out of Sync

Marshall's early college years were the last time when he might plausibly be described as average. Aside from being taller and skinnier than most students—and along with his proclivity for debating and his inventory of elocutionary reading skills—young Marshall was a fairly generic B+/A student as might be found on any North American campus of the era. He decided to study English literature.

The teaching of English literature in Winnipeg during the Depression was a dry, joyless activity. English departments were largely unaware of, and unconcerned with, the new modes of thinking about literature that were exploding in England: the New Criticism. Marshall intuited that his hometown was a place where a literary education was structured so that students accrued *petit bourgeois* culture by enjoying "the finer books in life." Literature studies then could be described as a highly programmatic Book-of-the-Month Club in disguise. New perspectives on the works of long-dead authors (or any perspectives on living ones) were not welcome.

Did this bug Marshall? Possibly a good deal. While he certainly disliked the modern world, he was always open to new ways of interpreting the Old World, especially if it involved hearing the echoes between one step toward modernity (like the print revolution) and another (like the electronic revolution). Marshall, in fact, pined for pre-modern, pre-technology times when people talked and didn't watch TV (he never took to it) and where books were read aloud in church by priests. Ironically, when he was demonized in later life, it was largely because his critics thought he was anti-book and pro-technology.

Marshall clearly didn't mind that the university focused on an inflexibly orthodox canon of writers. At one point he was even going to focus on nineteenth-century writers as his specialty. What Marshall *didn't* like about the writers he studied in university was the *manner* in which literature was taught and the way students were programmed to respond to it. He saw the teaching of criticism as being archaic, robotic, and ignorant of manifold viewpoints one might use to create a new interpretation of something old. He was determined to find new lenses through which to view the past—and to find new viewpoints that consolidated human experience into some kind of unified theory, quite possibly outside the realm of any orthodox theory. In this way he was entirely himself, even at a young age.

And in our mind's eye we have a vision of Marshall inhaling the contents of Michel Eyquem de Montaigne's *Essays,* internalizing them beside a fireplace on a sub-zero winter evening in almost the exact mathematical dead centre of North America in the third decade of the twentieth century.

Some of Marshall's courses at the University of Manitoba:[5]

History of Literature
Chaucer and Spenser
Shakespeare
Milton
Restoration and 18th-Century Literature
Victorian Poetry and Prose
Elementary Old English, Middle English and Advanced English
Drama
Non-dramatic Literature of the 16th and 17th Centuries
American, Contemporary and Canadian Poetry
Masterpieces of European Literature (including Homer, Plato, Virgil, Dante, Montaigne, Cervantes)

---

[5] All these writers are still studied, but it's hard to imagine living in a time and place when they were the *only* writers who were studied. I sometimes feel like an android from Mars when reading about what people in the past read, studied, and thought—to see what they were inflamed by, to see what they valued. The only rule of thumb is that academic regimes invariably come and go, denunciations are made, careers are destroyed, scores are settled, people die, someone's book gets made into a movie, vogues come and go, biographies mildew. Meanwhile, each new generation approaches the past like a box of Christmas decorations brought down from the attic: the curation of what survives operates by chains of events that rival the arbitrary selection and deletion processes used to assemble team members on TV reality shows.

Semi-Detached

Marshall's diaries as a university student reveal him to have been insecure around others, despite his cool demeanour, and puritanical—or perhaps chivalric—when it came to women, lacking basic knowledge about human sexuality. It was the Prairies and it was the Depression. People didn't discuss such things. His mother was his only model of feminine influence, and she was a walking bonfire. Elsie brought home girl after girl for Marshall, but what could be worse than a girl Elsie had chosen?

Disgusted by his feelings of lust, and avoiding dirty talk with the guys, he planned to marry, chaste, at thirty. He had a crush on teenaged American aviatrix Elinor Smith and wrote poems dedicated to her photo. He was clueless about how women thought or behaved. He was caught in a prude loop: any woman who succumbed to his lust couldn't possibly be the right sort of woman to be lusting after. He wasn't afraid of falling in love; rather, he was worried about falling in love with the wrong girl—a shallow girl. He didn't consider women to be the intellectual equivalents of men.

He played some rugby and hockey and (of course) relished debating. He had one good friend, Tom Easterbrook, and their favourite pastime was arguing.

The mind creates snapshots of this faraway time: Marshall spreading oily pesticides in mosquito breeding grounds as a summer job ... Marshall the dancer at a university social, having his pick of partners ... Marshall sailing his homemade model sailboat on the Red River ... Marshall riding a bus across town on a snowy day and seeing neon signs peeking out from foggy store windows ... Marshall alone in his room with a comically tall stack of books, methodically absorbing their contents as though they were drugs ... Marshall and Maurice arguing about God ... Marshall and Elsie arguing about Marshall's attitude ... Marshall cursing and trashing his mother in his diary ... Marshall cursing and trashing *himself* for thinking such things ... Marshall writing in his March 10, 1930, diary entry: "I must, must, must attain worldly success to a real degree" ... Elsie storming out the door, not to return for weeks or, possibly, forever.

Arrrrr!

In the summer of 1932, Marshall and his friend Tom had an adventure. They sailed to England on a cattle ship, tending to the animals on the night shift, Marshall spending the majority of the trip seasick.

The two friends had a hundred dollars apiece to last them three months, but they didn't care. Marshall, who had quite plausibly never seen anything built before 1900, was in a state of bliss: ancient things were everywhere, and with good luck, he could recite a nineteenth-century sonnet or ode to accompany the viewing experience. It wasn't so much a holiday as it was time travel, and it sealed the deal on Marshall's wish to return to England after university and study in the country he now considered his spiritual homeland.

Once back in Winnipeg, he discovered the writings of G.K. Chesterton, an early twentieth-century English writer Marshall was simultaneously drawn to and irked by. Both men hungered for a framework to make sense of the modern world. A famous "Chestertonism" (Chesterton loved aphorisms and mangled puns as much as Marshall did) goes: "The whole modern world has divided itself into Conservatives and Progressives. The business of Progressives is to go on making mistakes. The business of the Conservatives is to prevent the mistakes from being corrected." Nothing so clearly describes Marshall's own skeptical and rather crustily conservative attitude toward politics, an attitude he maintained across the span of his life and a subject he almost never discussed in public or private. If society is polarized by progress versus conservatism, there is no room for the eternal. Marshall's life and Chesterton's have much in common. Both men became Catholic converts in their thirties, and both had a whiff of the old fogey about them long before they were old.

In the end, Marshall ran hot and cool on Chesterton, as he would on other influential older figures in his life, such as Wyndham Lewis. These were Elsie-like relationships, involving the sort of reader-to-writer, junior-to-senior, love-to-hate equation one has when connecting to a person of authority who reminds one highly of oneself. In a way, this dynamic defines much of Marshall's relationship to literature and the media—in love with them, yet revolting against them.

Marshall continued his English studies at the University of Manitoba. He also took what had been the spark of a relationship with a girl and kindled it into a burning first love. The flame was Marjorie, a medical student two years older than he. That he would fall for a strong woman trying to make a go of it in a man's world is unsurprising. Marshall wrote love poems to Marjorie, with whom a physical attraction was reciprocal. This was certainly the period in his life when he went from being an asexual nerdy guy to being a guy with … *needs*. But, in the final and mutual analysis (which wouldn't happen until many years later), Marjorie was simply too old and Marshall too young. Given her projected career arc versus Marshall's, the match had a doomed aura that probably suited each quite well: it lifted them emotionally off the hook while they went about completing their respective steps toward success, as well as—importantly—getting their families off their backs in an era where a single woman at twenty-five was a spinster and a single man at twenty-five was an issue one didn't discuss at all.

Meanwhile, Elsie left Herbert for good, moving to Toronto in 1933 to go it alone—no divorce, rather simple abandonment. She took Maurice with her, leaving a distinctly quieter household on Gertrude Street behind her, but with it a lingering mist of female rage, female contempt for males, and a succession of useless, archaic ideologies and religious beliefs that had neither helped nor saved anybody.

Marshall by then saw that his path to success was going to be in academics, and literary studies at Cambridge was the ideal first step. He applied for a memorial scholarship funded by the Daughters of the Empire to encourage promising colonials to develop their intellect in the refining fire of a British university.[6] But one of the adjudicators was a professor whom Marshall had ticked off throughout his years of being a classroom nuisance, with his incessant interjections

---

[6] In the 1930s, when North American students went to Cambridge and Oxford for an undergraduate degree, they had to already have one from North America just to qualify. They were then allowed to get their English bachelor's on an accelerated program. Patronizing? *Oui.*

and corrections. Marshall knew his impulsive behaviour had come back to bite him, but this time it was Herbert, not Elsie, who came to his rescue, visiting the prof and using his charm and bonhomie to squeak Marshall past the finish line.

The thesis that landed Marshall the scholarship was on the work of George Meredith, a nineteenth-century writer who dealt with the mind and how it learns. Marshall liked Meredith because "he couldn't be placed," and he noted elsewhere that Meredith had "no derivation and no tendency; and yet he bridges the gap between 18th and 20th centuries as if the Victorian era had never been."

The same might be said about Marshall. The world he described didn't really become manifest until the twenty-first century and the rise of the internet. The twentieth century was a progressively bad dream he dismissed in order to bridge the reign of Queen Victoria over and across to the reign of Google.

Life mimics art. But in the broadest of senses, one might actually say that Marshall's ideas intellectually connected the Renaissance with the twenty-first century—from the Gutenberg print revolution and the scientific revolution it triggered to the Google-ous twenty-first century, skipping everything in between except Pound and Joyce (who were building similar bridges themselves).

> He found words for his treasure-house ... at haphazard in the shops, on advertisements, in the mouths of the plodding public. He kept repeating them to himself till they lost all instantaneous meaning for him and became wonderful vocables.
>
> James Joyce

A Quirky Lad from the Colonies

Cambridge in the 1930s was, for an anglophile like Marshall, a dream within a dream. The university's dominant ideological battles revolved around Freudianism and new philosophical systems such as those of Wittgenstein, Russell, Whitehead, and Marx. In the English faculty, the New Criticism was bull-dozing existing modes of literary discussion. Marshall's instructor at Cambridge was I.A. Richards, a psychologist turned literary critic. Richards wrote a book entitled *Practical Criticism* in 1929, beginning a new wave of literary criticism now known as New Criticism, which was the dominant trend in English and American literary criticism from the 1920s to

---

[7] Okay, as much of this information came from Wikipedia, this is a good moment to tell my Wikipedia story. I was watching Sofia Coppola's *Marie Antoinette* on DVD and after about two minutes I realized I needed a refresher course on Louis XVI. So I Wikipedia'ed him and printed out the results. I went back to the sofa and began reading the printout, which, on the third page, said, "Unknown to most people, Louis XVI and Marie Antoinette also had a fourth child, a male whose skin was so plasticky and shiny looking that he was shipped to North America where he was adopted

the early 1960s that peaked in the 1940s and 1950s.[7] The proponents of the New Criticism believed that all that counted were the words on the paper. Knowledge of the author, his or her life, the context of the words—all other factors—was irrelevant. The New Criticism focused on understanding how lit-

---

by acclaimed American film director, Paul Thomas Anderson." The entry spun onward from there, and to read it was a mind-blowing experience, like I'd accidentally slipped into the subconscious of global culture, like seeing what machines dream about.

Needless to say, it's not hard to guess that Marshall would be appalled and horrified by Wikipedia, and not just because it's a relatively new technology and hence must be reflexively loathed. Rather, Wikipedia is one more incarnation of the internet world where language is corrupted, eventually leading to a dystopic future. (Question: Is the future ever *not* dystopic? And thank heaven librarians as well as vandals troll the internet to fix errors and inconsistencies.)

On the other hand, here's the thing: it doesn't matter whether I, as a biographer, drive to the civic library and hang out with the reference librarians all day—in the end, I'd end up with the same information that I'd have found here at home, online. Would the bricks-and-mortar research come with a pedigree? Would I need to show Chevron gas slips and document my mileage to score points? This throws the notion of "biography" into a new light. We can all hopscotch from link to link to link—it's what most people do now, anyway. So why write a biography? Maybe to get a sense of how it felt to be someone else in a different time. Maybe to cast new light on an old subject. Maybe to learn new ways of thinking. Maybe to try to enter an already vanishing mode of perceiving the past, the notion that a landscape is best viewed with a single source of light—the sun, one light bulb, a lone candle, a lone writer—so that all the shadows and highlights are true to each other.

erature achieved its effect on readers. Marshall came to believe that the content of a poem, for instance, was derived from how its words worked together in a formal context, not from the author's intent. It was F.R. Leavis[8] who, uncharacteristically for the times, encouraged Marshall to study the real world with the same sort of lens used to view the literary world. Decades later, astonishing results bloomed from this advice. In the short term, exposure to the New Criticism rescued Marshall from the archaic mush of a Depression-era Manitoban education and propelled him into reading authors he'd never before considered, such as Joyce, Eliot, and Yeats.

The New Criticism fed Marshall's natural tendency to be open to listening to any new idea. It allowed him to look at a poem, say, as an artifact inside a glass case. And to a rabid learner of obscure words, the New Criticism gave Marshall impetus to continue exploring the physical sensations of reading—the sensations of the throat, tongue, and lips— ultimately arriving at a place where he could play with a single word for hours, toying with its richness and nuances. He once said that a single word in the English language was

---

[8] Frank Raymond Leavis CH (July 14, 1895–April 14, 1978) was an influential British literary critic of the early to mid-twentieth century. He taught and studied for nearly his entire life at Downing College, Cambridge. (Wikipedia)

more complex than the U.S. space program. An exaggeration, but it made a point (here we are, discussing it half a century later), and such overstatements always landed him publicity, something he loved his whole life in a sweet, uncynical, and innocent way. *(Look, Ma!)*

A special note about this period of Marshall's Cambridge life is the influence of Alfred North Whitehead, then at Harvard, a thinker whose influence reached its acme in the 1950s and 1960s. Whitehead's aphorisms are pencilled all over Marshall's papers, and to read a few of them is to have a preview of the places Marshall would visit in the years to come:

> The silly question is the first intimation of some totally new development.
> Alfred North Whitehead

> Fundamental progress has to do with the reinterpretation of basic ideas.
> Alfred North Whitehead

> Civilization advances by extending the number of important operations which we can perform without thinking of them.
> Alfred North Whitehead

The Canuck Savant

By 1934 Marshall's brain had become more fully wired, making him far more gregarious than he had been in his youth. He was a terrific debater, and his ability to elocute masses of poetry and prose pre-empted his detractors from treating him like a bumpkin.

His day-to-day needs were met with cozy Old World accommodations and regular meals. He was on the rowing team. He didn't have a girlfriend. He liked watching detective films at a local cinema. He wrote letters home almost daily. He was earnest. He became hungrier and hungrier for religion—Elsie had always sensed in her son what she called a "religion-hunting tendency," and this need was hitting a tipping point. Specifically, it was Marshall's enthusiasm for G.K. Chesterton and his blossoming relationships with Catholic friends that allowed him to steer away from his Protestant prairie upbringing. To him, Protestant-themed religions meant cheap houses, billboards, spraying dirt ditches with pesticides for thirty cents an hour—plus the absence of most forms of high culture. Catholicism offered Rome! History! Art! Beauty! Ritual! But most of all, it allowed Marshall a spot to park his overpowering need for a viewpoint that could explain, or perhaps heal, the stress and disjointedness he saw in the world.

When the Road Forks

Depending on your beliefs, a lot of things can happen after you die. Perhaps nothing happens. Perhaps you reincarnate. (Marshall found that idea ludicrous.) Or maybe you enter eternity. But if you enter eternity, what happens to the world you left behind? How do you explain the fact that, while you're busy hanging out in eternity, the world you left behind has merely the drab little *future* ahead of it? Eternity is not the future, nor vice versa. Although he never phrased it as such, it was the irreconcilability of the world with the afterworld that generated the contradictions that defined much of Marshall's career. On the one hand, technology was a bauble played within the mortal coil. It was not worthy of the respect accorded religion. On the other, it was a transformative agent for the mind and for society. It had to be worthy of the same attention as literature. It was this detachment from the worldly that afforded him an objectivity missing in other social analysts. Constant awareness of the ancient and divine allowed him an unsentimental perspective on the technical and cultural, and on both the modern age and its future. The world was merely the world. Because of this, he tended to find similarities when comparing one era with another, rather than looking only for differences. Add to this his innate gift for spotting broad patterns (some so broad that they take fifty years to be proven accurate), and snapshots of the man emerge.

The New Spectrum

Marshall exhibited throughout his life a certain sense of obliviousness about the physical world—he was the epitome of the absent-minded professor. He couldn't drive a car. His environments were in shambles. He tuned in and out of conversations with friends and strangers, and during classes would ramble, seemingly unaware of those around him, clicking in and out of reality. Many people, when describing their encounters with him, say that with Marshall you had a few seconds to say your hellos or make your point, and after that he was back on Planet Marshall. And this is not to confuse obliviousness with cluelessness. Marshall had created a rich inner life. Why leave it if he didn't have to?

Perhaps this disassociation, along with others of Marshall's traits, should be placed on an autistic spectrum. This can actually be said of anyone on earth. Autism is no longer a binary diagnosis but is, rather, a spectral condition within which everyone exists, as they do within the depressive and schizophrenic spectrums. For example, there was Marshall's hypersensitivity to noise and sounds—loud and/or sudden and/or unwanted.[9] The man disliked disruption of daily patterns. He disliked being touched or jostled. He loved ritual. He punned (punning is a form of disinhibition related to neural wiring in the brain's limbic system). Marshall, like many writers (manic or not), enjoyed what

---

[9] I quit smoking on Halloween 1988. In December 1988 I was walking to work in a snowstorm when I had the biggest sneeze of my life and afterwards found in my hand a clump of living tissue the size, shape, and colour of a Thompson seedless green grape. It had veins. Of course this freaked me out, and I went right to a doctor, who said that I should actually be thankful, because "At least it's not inside you any more." He made sense. But from that morning on, my hearing became hyperacute and hasn't wavered since. It's not just noises (of any sort) that shut me down (and by "shut me down," I mean they stop my body in mid-motion). Leaf blowers and hammers are the worst. But after the morning of the nasal incident, I also lost my ability to focus sounds. Restaurants are the worst. Or people in Europe who use cellphones on trains—people who use their outdoor voices indoors. I carry cards in my wallet to this effect. They read, I AM UNABLE TO "FOCUS" SOUND AND AM UNABLE TO HEAR YOU PROPERLY. PLEASE HAVE PATIENCE. I hand them out mostly to airline employees and hotel front desk staff. At first, they tend to think I'm running a charity scam, and then they realize I'm for real. I no longer attend large events that take place in big rooms. Also, in the 7,000 or so nights since then, I've not once been able to sleep without earplugs, and at its very worst, in 1993, I couldn't stay in hotels or do any work of any sort until late at night and into the early morning, when most people are asleep. So when I found out that Marshall's hearing went cuckoo after they took a lump out of his head, I said, "Yes, this is someone I want to write a biography about."

are called *clang associations.*[10] Marshall was also obsessed with words and memorization, and he was, it has been said, *oblivious*—not cripplingly so, but it did alter his ability to communicate in person in a way that, if nothing else, probably didn't help him. Older people interpreted his obliviousness as arrogance; young people interpreted it as cool.

This is not to say that Marshall was autistic, or even a high-functioning Asperger syndrome autistic. But if he had any specific psychopathology, that would be the direction in which to look. He wasn't depressive. He wasn't schizophrenic. He wasn't addicted to alcohol or anything else. He was, to an admirable degree, a happy man with a great family and career. But he *did* tend to be curiously and creatively oblivious. As his biographer Philip Marchand says,

> If he had a weakness, it was his inability to listen to speakers less forceful than he was. His forte, on the other hand, was talking tirelessly not only in brilliantly articulate sentences but whole paragraphs—a form of communication he much preferred to writing.

---

[10] Clang associations are formally defined as "psychic associations resulting from sounds, often observed in the manic phase of manic-depressive psychosis." In simpler terms, clang associations are groupings of words based on their sounds, generally rhyming or partially rhyming, without there necessarily being any logical reason to put them together. (www.about.com)

Perhaps this opens the door to what may be one future for the biography of those who create new ideas, a form in which the biographer mixes historical circumstances with forensic medical diagnosis to create what might be called a *pathography*—an attempt to map a subject's brain functions and to chart the way they create what we call the self. Marshall lived in the age of lobotomies and barbiturates. Now, a hundred years after his birth, we have PET scans, MRI imaging, gene mapping, and a tsunami of research into psychopharmacology, as well as informed new ways of explaining the human condition as it is affected by the structure and chemistry of the brain. Ironically, the brain was the subject of McLuhan's own last, long inquiry. More on that later.

The AQ Test

Psychologist Simon Baron-Cohen[11] and his colleagues at Cambridge's Autism Research Centre have created the Autism-Spectrum Quotient, or AQ, as a measure of the extent of autistic traits in adults. In the first major trial using the test, the average score in the control group was 16.4. Eighty percent of those diagnosed with autism or a related disorder scored 32 or higher. The test is not a means for making a diagnosis, however, and many who score above 32 and even meet the diagnostic criteria for mild autism or Asperger's report no difficulty functioning in their everyday lives.

Definitely agree
      Slightly agree
            Slightly disagree
                  Definitely disagree

1   I prefer to do things with others rather than on my own.

2   I prefer to do things the same way over and over again.

3   If I try to imagine something, I find it very easy to create a picture in my mind.

4   I frequently get so strongly absorbed in one thing that I lose sight of other things.

---

[11] Yes, Simon is a first cousin of Sasha Baron-Cohen of *Borat* and *Brüno* fame.

5   I often notice small sounds when others do not.

6   I usually notice car number plates or similar strings of information.

7   Other people frequently tell me that what I've said is impolite, even though I think it is polite.

8   When I'm reading a story, I can easily imagine what the characters might look like.

9   I am fascinated by dates.

10 In a social group, I can easily keep track of several different people's conversations.

11 I find social situations easy.

12 I tend to notice details that others do not.

13 I would rather go to a library than to a party.

14 I find making up stories easy.

15 I find myself drawn more strongly to people than to things.

16 I tend to have very strong interests, which I get upset about if I can't pursue.

17 I enjoy social chitchat.

18 When I talk, it isn't always easy for others to get a word in edge-wise.

19 I am fascinated by numbers.

20 When I'm reading a story, I find it difficult to work out the characters' intentions.

21 I don't particularly enjoy reading fiction.

22 I find it hard to make new friends.

23 I notice patterns in things all the time.

24 I would rather go to the theater than to a museum.

25 It does not upset me if my daily routine is disturbed.

26 I frequently find that I don't know how to keep a conversation going.

27 I find it easy to "read between the lines" when someone is talking to me.

28 I usually concentrate more on the whole picture, rather than on the small details.

29 I am not very good at remembering phone numbers.

30 I don't usually notice small changes in a situation or a person's appearance.

31 I know how to tell if someone listening to me is getting bored.

32 I find it easy to do more than one thing at once.

33 When I talk on the phone, I'm not sure when it's my turn to speak.

34 I enjoy doing things spontaneously.

35 I am often the last to understand the point of a joke.

36 I find it easy to work out what someone is thinking or feeling just by looking at their face.

37 If there is an interruption, I can switch back to what I was doing very quickly.

38 I am good at social chitchat.

39 People often tell me that I keep going on and on about the same thing.

40 When I was young, I used to enjoy playing games involving pretending with other children.

41 I like to collect information about categories of things (e.g., types of cars, birds, trains, plants).

42 I find it difficult to imagine what it would be like to be someone else.

43 I like to carefully plan any activities I participate in.

44 I enjoy social occasions.

45 I find it difficult to work out people's intentions.

46 New situations make me anxious.

47 I enjoy meeting new people.

48 I am a good diplomat.

49 I am not very good at remembering people's date of birth.

50 I find it very easy to play games with children that involve pretending.

How to score: "Definitely agree" or "Slightly agree" responses to questions 2, 4, 5, 6, 7, 9, 12, 13, 16, 18, 19, 20, 21, 22, 23, 26, 33, 35, 39, 41, 42, 43, 45, 46 score 1 point.

"Definitely disagree" or "Slightly disagree" responses to questions 1, 3, 8, 10, 11, 14, 15, 17, 24, 25, 27, 28, 29, 30, 31, 32, 34, 36, 37, 38, 40, 44, 47, 48, 49, 50 score 1 point.

In America, low, middle and high are consumer ratings, and nothing more. But woe to the indigent intellectual who acquires a "high" rating without the economic appendages. He is undermining the system.

M.M.

Perhaps the world has been given to us as an anti-environment to make us aware of [God's] word.

M.M.

Marshall's America

Marshall received his second B.A., from Cambridge, in the summer of 1936. He gained only second-class honours, so his scholarship could not be renewed, and he set about looking for a job. But during his two English years he'd been close to the inner core of emerging twentieth-century critical theory. He'd become more of a man and less of a youth. He'd inhaled countless books. He'd toured France in his off time. He'd compared the Old World to the New and found he much preferred the Old. He had filled out a bit. He'd grown a moustache. But, now unemployed, he was entering a period of rootlessness and misdirection that almost anybody who's ever graduated from school knows all too well. Marshall looked for a college situation that offered any form of stability and coherence, not easy in the Depression years. He even applied to teach at his nemesis, the University of Manitoba, an unsuccessful application that would have meant a huge psychic step backward. He ended up as a teaching assistant at the University of Wisconsin, in Madison, earning $895 a month. With his first paycheque, he bought a briefcase and a steak.

Madison, though touted as the Athens of the west, was a world away from Cambridge, and that distance from the patterns of discourse he knew came to post-England

Marshall as a shell shock. Before the Second World War, the United States and Canada were still markedly different from each other. Canada was an imperial dominion, the inheritor of Britain's oligarchic system of finance, politics, and culture, and its educational system was steeped in imitations of the British. U.S. culture was, as it is now, one of hard-core capitalism married to mass marketing and scientific research, spawning a breed of civilization that was marked by ambition: money-driven, results-based, focused on the current, and, for lack of a better word, *peppier* than Canada's. American secular universities, especially in the Midwest, were based on a "positivist" model borrowed from Germany and France, more concerned about communicating information than ideas. These schools were pragmatic, focused on scientific truth, not moral or theoretical debate. Marshall was only a few years older than his students, but those students might as well have hailed from Alpha Centauri. They spoke in slang, knew little of history and almost nothing of the cultures of the past. To Marshall, they lived in a perpetual present and saw nothing wrong with that.

How could these products of a similar culture seven hundred miles from Winnipeg have created students so alien? McLuhan felt he had no common language to speak with his students, as if the culture he came from was governed by completely different references and forces. Despairing at this lack of a common language, he radicalized his thinking and teaching. He decided to use the notion of his old professor, Cambridge's F.R. Leavis—the idea that all realms of culture, not merely literary works, are open to theoretical analysis. Thus, Marshall set about deconstructing mass culture. At first, it was simply a means of trying to cross an otherwise uncrossable cultural canyon, but at the same time, observing his students, he also became interested in exploring the way people learn to perceive their worlds, starting to recognize how the media one learns from go on first to subtly manipulate the information they present, and then to rewire the way the mind configures that information—and all other information.

To get a grasp of both matters, he began a campaign of reading that formed the nucleus of his future leaps: Joyce, Pound, Eliot, as well as the philosophy—especially the work of Alfred North Whitehead—that he had been exposed to at Cambridge.

On the other hand, in Madison Marshall also found a highly American sort of "bullshitty" collegiality and camaraderie. He grew to love the word *bullshit*, as well as the idea of *bullshitting* and throwing ideas around in casual banter as a means of generating new ideas. Nonetheless, Marshall was

a stranger in a strange land, and he was lonely. He partici-
pated in debates and arguments, but he felt isolated.

> Let your religion be less of a theory and more of a love affair.
> G.K. Chesterton

> The total absence of humor from the Bible is one
> of the most singular things in all literature.
> Alfred North Whitehead

God and Man

And so there was a lonely young Marshall in a foreign city,
teaching students he considered space aliens. He knew that
seven hundred miles away, his family was in the final stages
of disintegration; whether by choice or by fate, he was still
single and had nobody with whom to share his life.

It was at this point that a letter arrived from Father
Gerald Phelan, president of the Pontifical Institute of
Medieval Studies at St. Michael's College at the University of
Toronto. Phelan had read an article by Marshall on
Chesterton that had appeared in a university quarterly. The
two began a correspondence, and, during Christmas 1936,
while visiting Elsie in Toronto, Marshall met with Phelan,
who was, coincidentally, an acquaintance of Elsie's. Her
motherly Geiger counter must surely have been bleeping off
the dial to see her religion-hunting son Marshall falling into

the clutches of the Catholics. In any event, his meeting with Phelan must have gone well. The lonely young man returned to America and, on Tuesday, March 30, 1937, was received into the Church.

Marshall's conversion devastated the ambitious Elsie, who considered the move "career suicide." She blamed Herbert's side of the family and was miserable. This was twenty-six years before John F. Kennedy was elected president, less than a decade since the Ku Klux Klan had marched against Catholic New York governor Al Smith. Catholics were still viewed as pawns of the Vatican and widely mistrusted in a dominantly Protestant continent.

Marshall, like most converts, quickly became hard core. He went to Mass almost every day for the rest of his life. He recited the rosary. He was a firm believer in Hell. He was disgusted that other Catholics weren't Catholic enough. Above all, he believed that because God made the world, it must, in the end, be comprehensible, and that a sense of the divine could lead to an understanding of the mundane. He came to feel that his religion was indeed a sense, a sensory perception that coloured his life as much as, if not more so than, sight, taste, touch, hearing, smell, or gravity. He'd found his key to eternity and was now free to turn his full and detached attention to the merely human and societal "future." The future, compared to Heaven, was downmarket, to be viewed dispassionately, as though prognosticating an ant farm, a kind of acutely observant obliviousness.

Marshall didn't publicly discuss his religion. His theory was that people who can see don't walk around saying, "I'm seeing things" all day. They simply see the world. And so, with religion, it was simply there with him. This unwillingness to discuss religion caused him much trouble. Some people perceived it as arrogance. Some people saw it as weakness and shirking. Some people saw it as outdated and ridiculous. Some saw it as a wasted chance to make converts.

> I wouldn't have seen it if I hadn't believed it.
> M.M.

Forming a Posse

Bored with the U of W's noxious political infighting, depressed by his historically blank students, and eager to make his life more Catholic, and quickly, Marshall applied to the Catholic Saint Louis University, where the head of the literature department, William McCabe, was a Cambridge graduate and surprisingly up to date on developments in the field. Marshall was accepted as a full instructor at three times his Wisconsin pay.

Shortly thereafter, in the summer of 1937, Marshall spent a few weeks with Elsie on Vancouver Island. At the end of the trip, he and Elsie took the train back east—Marshall as far as Winnipeg, and Elsie continuing on to Toronto.

Elsie and Herbert hadn't seen or spoken to each other in three years, and on the platform in Winnipeg they spoke civilly for one hour. Then Elsie got back on the train and was gone.

Marshall spent three weeks in his old house, with Herbert and without his brother, and then left for St. Louis.

St. Louis University was a good gig. Dating back to 1818, it was one of the oldest Jesuit colleges in America. Well established (if a little decrepit), it neatly suited Marshall: one hundred percent male, tweedy, and unstylish. It followed the Jesuit ideal that the divine can be revealed (and this is *truly* critical to Marshall's later life) and the doctrine of the Church made knowable through *probing, provocation, open discussion, analysis, debate,* and *inquiry*—rather the opposite of Chesterton's belief that religion should be a love affair.

Marshall quickly came to enjoy the city and the company of his fellow faculty members, many of whom became life-long friends and collaborators. He had a posse of colleagues who could deal with him on a high intellectual level and on the same theological plane. Along with Father William

McCabe, there was Father Walter Ong, a young Jesuit whom Marshall tutored. There was Bernard Muller-Thym, a philosophy instructor completing his Ph.D. for the University of Toronto's Pontifical Institute of Medieval Studies. And there was Felix Giovanelli, a language instructor who would later collaborate with Marshall. These men, along with his old Manitoba friend Tom Easterbrook, were the first members of Marshall's personal proto–Warhol Factory, whose ideas helped codify and articulate the genesis of Media Theory that would explode in 1962.

49° North

Americans and Canadians crossed the border more freely then, unhindered by citizenship or paperwork. In England, Marshall was a novelty; in Saint Louis, being Canadian meant nothing. He once said that it was the prairie skies of his youth that made him look forward into the future, but that sense of vista was more geographical than geopolitical. It is helpful to understand, though, the way a young Marshall may have perceived space, coming from a land where all people were far apart from all other people, where travel of any sort involved provisions for weather, duration, and discomfort. Picture a young Marshall wondering where his mother was at any given moment, off in the endless flatness, off beyond the horizon that never ends. Imagine Elsie writing letters and those letters being placed into canvas bags and loaded into train cars and delivered days later, with young Marshall contemplating the distance from which they came. Imagine bad, crackly telephone lines and scratchy and limited radio ... and nothing else. Imagine the minds of Marshall and others of his era, always thinking about the relationship between distance and speed. Imagine the ongoing familial parade of rootless religious mutts, always pulling up stakes and moving from one chunk of godforsaken flatness to a newer chunk of flatness, with God laughing all the way. Imagine what it was like to come from a place in the middle of the continent, the middle of nowhere, always wishing you could be somewhere. Imagine Elsie pulling out of the Winnipeg railway station, vanishing into the horizon, probably quite thrilled to have her one-hour encounter with Herbert over with, and quite possibly reciting a love sonnet to nobody (or perhaps somebody) in particular. And that's a part of Marshall's upbringing.

The Marshall we find in 1937 in St. Louis was a skinny guy who seemed prematurely old, who talked only about religion and literature, who had no listening skills, and who would probably have tuned you out the moment he determined that you weren't bombastic—a personality trait

Marshall found irresistible, the one trait that might make him stop and listen fully to another person. *This* was the guru whose ideas would revolutionize the way we see the universe?

But then we read a letter Marshall wrote to his brother, Maurice, about his life at that time, and it shows within the emerging fuddy-duddy a burning white core ...

> What I am now, I must be, more or less, for the rest of my life, and it gives me a queer feeling of hopelessness to think that all those large dreams of the powers and talents which I was to possess at this time for the bedazzlement of men and perhaps the "bedazzlement of Heaven with high astounding terms" are just a chimerical blank. I have no affection for the world. I cannot be sure whether my present indifference to its objectives and pleasures is genuinely grounded in the love of God or merely in the despair of myself. At least I can say this, that my dissatisfaction is so deep that I cannot imagine anyone in history or anyone alive who I would choose to be (saints excepted because they weren't trying to collect from life) rather than myself.

... and with it a sense that the man to be was now complete. Marshall had become McLuhan.

The Trivium

In medieval universities, the trivium comprised the three subjects taught first: grammar, logic, and rhetoric. The word is a Latin term meaning "the three ways" or "the three roads." The study of the trivium was considered preparatory for the quadrivium (arithmetic, geometry, music, and astronomy).

Grammar means written texts of all sorts, both sacred and profane, as well as (and this is important for Marshall) the *world* and the *entire known universe*, which were considered as a book. It is the mechanics of a language, of inventing symbols and combining them to express thought.

Dialectic (or logic) is the "mechanics" of thought and analysis, the art of thinking—philosophy.

Rhetoric is the use of language to instruct and persuade. It is the art of communicating thought from one mind to another, the adaptation of language to circumstance. Rhetoric is concerned with the thing as it is communicated.

St. Louis, Missouri

In St. Louis, Marshall was working toward his Cambridge doctorate (known in Britain as a D.Phil., not Ph.D.) on the work of an obscure sixteenth-century English pamphleteer, Thomas Nashe. That Marshall ended up becoming what he became as the result of studying a sixteenth-century English satirist, rhetorician, and critic is as freaky as if he'd studied Easter rituals in medieval France and emerged at the end as a rocket scientist.

His teaching load was massive, but it was good in Depression-era America simply to have a job, and the range of subjects he needed to teach forced him to keep reading new material, digest it, and process it at extraordinary speed, often almost immediately before teaching a class. It was neocortical gymnastics of the best sort—the dendrites and axons of his nearly completely wired brain were being thrown massive numbers of ideas, all of which helped configure his brain with the highest possible number of infraneural links. Had he stayed in engineering at the University of Manitoba, his brain would not have been the same. This is why we have good schools and must feed the minds of the young, and Marshall knew it.

St. Louis University was where Marshall learned that he liked an audience and that an audience liked him. His

courses were full and often audited, as he displayed his signature ability to juggle eleven idea balls at once. Any doubts
about whether he would be a teacher were squelched. In
St. Louis, Marshall also continued his lifelong tendency to
over-research his areas of inquiry. Aside from reading books
required for teaching, he was reading works on the language,
thought, and literature of Shakespearean England recommended to him by William McCabe, so as to get a handle
on Nashe. The inside of Marshall's head must have felt as
though it was filled with exploding Roman candles.

He studied the intellectual history of the Middle Ages
and the Renaissance. He talked a lot about God with a lot of
people. He began thinking about how the body absorbs
information and about how the brain sees and interprets
words and noises. He wrote articles that scathed godless
modes of authority such as Marxism, capitalism, the modern
state, and advertising.

At the same time, as the mind began to heat up with new
inquiries, the man began to thaw out a bit, to become a bit
less priggish and a bit friendlier. He enjoyed himself for a
year, but there was a dash of *tristesse* to this enjoyment, as he
enjoyed it alone; it really had become time for him to meet
a future Mrs. McLuhan.

Enter Elsie, who, in 1938, was in California, studying at the Pasadena Playhouse, close to the Huntington Library in San Marino, which had vital material on the life of Thomas Nashe.

A point of view can be a dangerous luxury when substituted for insight and understanding.
M.M.

An administrator in a bureaucratic world is a man who can feel big by merging his non-entity in an abstraction. A real person in touch with real things inspires terror in him.
M.M.

Art is anything you can get away with.
M.M.

The Unmechanical Bride

It really is a chicken-and-egg proposition to wonder which came first, the Playhouse or the Huntington. Regardless, the coincidence of geographies brought Marshall conveniently close to Elsie, who was in good form. She was busy and had people around her and wasn't in her Herbert-castigating mode. She had also chosen the right girl for Marshall. Her name was Corinne Keller Lewis, a graduate of Texas Christian University, one year younger than Marshall. Corinne had worked as a drama teacher in Fort Worth and was an aspiring actress at the Pasadena Playhouse. Her genteel Southern family's name and money was made by the manufacture of buggies.

Corinne was a universally liked woman, engaging and warm to the same extent that Marshall was oblivious and without temperature. After an introduction from Elsie, the pair enjoyed a montage-like sequence of blossoming love in Los Angeles, visiting Catalina and hiking the city's hills under blue skies.

When it came time to go back to St. Louis, a lovestruck Marshall freaked out, for lack of a better term. His feelings for Corinne were different from those he'd had for his Winnipeg quasi-girlfriend-of-mutual-convenience, the medical student Marjorie. Marshall and Corinne traded letters (the email of their day) daily. Marshall's letters were earnest and (to Corinne) could have been a bit more romantic. Her family went way back to the plantation era, and they weren't happy about Marshall butting into the picture they'd painted for themselves of Corinne's future. Marshall was Catholic, of a lineage unfamiliar to them, not rich—and kind of weird. There were no overlaps between their universe and his. During the Christmas break of 1938, Marshall checked into a Fort Worth hotel to hound Corinne in person. His future mother-in-law grudgingly threw a drinks party and left it at that. Marshall went back to St. Louis more freaked out and lovesick than ever.

In June 1939, he visited Corinne in Texas and gave her a now legendary ultimatum that she frequently referred to: he was headed to Cambridge that fall to work on his thesis, and unless she consented to marry him at once, their relationship would have to end. She agreed to marry him before the end of August. She gathered a hurried trousseau and went to St. Louis, where she married Marshall in a Catholic church. Shortly after that, they took an ocean liner to England, settling in Cambridge with exceptionally odd timing. They landed on September 2, 1939, the day the Second World War began. England and Canada were at war with Germany, but for Marshall, his year in Cambridge with Corinne was enchanted—they had each other and they had culture and a good life together.

Marshall was also deeply engrossed in researching his dissertation on the rhetoric of Thomas Nashe. To ramp up to Nashe, though, involved a huge study of rhetoric, from the Greeks to the Renaissance. In doing this, he became interested in the manner in which different types of written and oral speech have affected the lives of civilizations. This interest then morphed into a broader subject: the influence of all kinds of communications media on individual consciousness, and how those individual changes might collectively change society.

... command
... shift

Loveable Light Gal
Loveable Lag Light
Bagel Voltage Hill
Gable Voltage Hill
Labile Haggle Volt
Liable Haggle Volt
Tillable Gavel Hog
Tillable Gag Hovel
Tillable Hag Glove
Livable Haggle Lot
Viable Haggle Toll
Viable Hall Toggle
Label Alight Glove
Lovable Haggle Lit
Lovable Gale Light
Lovable Lethal Gig
Lovable Alight Leg
Lovable Alight Gel
Lovable Gall Eight
Ballet Haggle Viol
Ballet Village Hog
Global Leave Light
Global Gavel Lithe
Global Lethal Give
Global Halve Legit
Global Gall Thieve
Blah Tillage Glove
Bath Illegal Glove
Baht Illegal Glove
Ball Haggle Violet
Ballot Haggle Veil
Ballot Haggle Live
Ballot Haggle Evil
Ballot Haggle Vile
Ballot Hall Veggie

Allege Oval Blight
Haggle Oval Billet
Illegal Gavel Both
Tillage Halve Glob
Village Legal Both
Village Lethal Gob
Village Lethal Bog
Village Lathe Glob
Village Hall Begot
Village Lath Globe
Village Halt Globe
Voltage Hall Bilge
Gavel Hallo Giblet
Lethal Vial Boggle
Lathe Villa Boggle
Baa Level Light Log
Baa Glove Hell Gilt
Baa Glove Ell Light
Labia Egg Hell Volt
Algae Beg Hill Volt
Algae Big Hell Volt
Algae Glob Vet Hill
Agave Beg Hill Toll
Agave Beg Hilt Loll
Agave Bell Hog Lilt
Agave Bell Hog Till
Agave Bell Gill Hot
Agave Bell Log Hilt
Agave Bell Got Hill
Agave Bell Tog Hill
Agave Belt Log Hill
Agave Big Hell Toll
Agave Glib Hell Lot
Agave Glib The Loll
Agave Glob Hell Lit

Agave Glob Ell Hilt
Agave Glob Let Hill
Agave Gob Hell Lilt
Agave Gob Hell Till
Agave Gob Tell Hill
Agave Bog Hell Lilt
Agave Bog Hell Till
Agave Bog Tell Hill
Agave Hob Tell Gill
Agave Both Ell Gill
Agave Bill Hell Got
Agave Bill Hell Tog
Agave Bill Tell Hog
Agave Boll Leg Hilt
Agave Boll Gel Hilt
Agave Boll Get Hill
Agave Boll The Gill
Agave Lob Hell Gilt
Agave Lob Ell Light
Agave Blot Leg Hill
Agave Blot Gel Hill
Agave Bolt Leg Hill
Agave Bolt Gel Hill
Gaga Bevel Hill Lot
Gaga Bevel Hit Loll
Gaga Bile Hell Volt
Gaga Vibe Hell Toll
Gaga Bell Hive Toll
Gaga Bell Hovel Lit
Gaga Bell Hove Lilt
Gaga Bell Hove Till
Gaga Bell Love Hilt
Gaga Bell Vole Hilt
Gaga Bell Veto Hill
Gaga Bell Vote Hill

Gaga Belt Hive Loll
Gaga Belt Hell Viol
Gaga Belt Hovel Ill
Gaga Belt Love Hill
Gaga Belt Vole Hill
Gaga Hob Level Lilt
Gaga Hob Level Till
Gaga Both Level Ill
Gaga Lib Helve Toll
Gaga Lib Hovel Tell
Gaga Bill Heel Volt
Gaga Bill Helve Lot
Gaga Bill Level Tho
Gaga Bill Level Hot
Gaga Bill Hell Veto
Gaga Bill Hell Vote
Gaga Bill Hello Vet
Gaga Bill Hovel Let
Gaga Bill Hove Tell
Gaga Bit Helve Loll
Gaga Boll Helve Lit
Gaga Boll Level Hit
Gaga Boll Hive Tell
Gaga Lob Helve Lilt
Gaga Lob Helve Till
Gaga Lob Level Hilt
Gaga Blot Helve Ill
Gaga Blot Hell Veil
Gaga Blot Hell Live
Gaga Blot Hell Evil
Gaga Blot Hell Vile
Gaga Bolt Helve Ill
Gaga Bolt Hell Veil
Gaga Bolt Hell Live
Gaga Bolt Hell Evil
Global Village The

Canada is the only country in the world that knows how to live without an identity.
M.M.

I don't necessarily agree with everything I say.
M.M.

Innumerable confusions and a feeling of profound despair invariably emerge in periods of great technological and cultural transition.
M.M.

That Was Us and This Is You

The year is 1940, and the twentieth century is four decades old, but it feels like it's only begun. You're living in St. Louis, Missouri, with a beautiful new wife. Your favourite meal is steak. You walk to work at the university to teach, and you see billboards selling crap: tires, nylons, paint, soup, golf balls, bacon—*anything*. Yet it's all a bit seductive: the breasts of the women never sag, and the men have boxers' torsos, and the otherworldly properties of the products are simply not to be believed. You want to point out some of the absurdities of these Technicolor pimpings, but you can't because people in schools don't discuss mass culture, and students don't care, because, *Why bother? It's merely advertising*. You've decided that advertising is an aesthetic experience, and yet it will be another fifteen years before the first signs of pop art seal that deal. If you survey the planet, there's no other art form out there in any culture—verbal or visual—that addresses mass culture in a way that is analytical and open-minded and generous when it needs to be. The Dadaists had worshiped urinals and snow shovels—at least they were open to new ideas. And the Cubists were at least willing to give new viewpoints a try, but it's been three decades now, so come on. Salvador Dali? He's *nuts* ... and a Freudian.

Moreover, nobody else on the planet, (then) population 2.5 billion, seems to have noticed: *Hey! There's something going on here with all these cheerleaders fellating Coke bottles and executives dropping trousers that never need ironing.* Strategies used to promote tyrants are being used to promote laundry soap. Unlucky you! *Unlucky you!* You're alone in the middle of a big, blank continent, walking to work, thinking you're crazy because nobody else can see that there's a sick beauty to all of these crappy, crappy ads that are *everywhere*. And the money that goes into them! The best and brightest minds bought and ransacked and poisoned by money. Well, now you're beginning to sound like a broken record, and there really is a part of your psyche wondering whether there's something damaged about you for believing that something above and beyond the obvious is going on with all these trashy-sexy ads that endlessly desecrate the landscape.

> When information is brushed up against information,
> the results are startling and effective.
> M.M.

> Almost all new ideas have a certain aspect of foolishness
> when they are first produced.
> Alfred North Whitehead

Bumstead!

Marshall and Corinne returned to St. Louis University in 1940. Marshall resumed teaching, but it wasn't the same as before. William McCabe had been replaced by the far less adventurous Norman Dreyfus, who couldn't stand McCabe and made life hell for any of his predecessor's protégés, mainly Marshall, who was assigned grunt jobs like teaching freshman English. And once the war came to the United States, late in 1941, Marshall was also enlisted for the war effort, made to teach report writing—inside tin huts and after school hours—to young women recruits.

There was a fundamental rift between Marshall and Dreyfus, the sort of schism in attitude and scholarly stance that followed Marshall throughout his career. McLuhan was notorious for deciding on the facts and finding the footnotes to support them later—a red cape brandished in the face of orthodox faculty toreadors. For Marshall, the fun of ideas lay in crashing them together to see what emerged from the collision. (Dear God, he would have enjoyed using the internet.)

Marshall was a quick reader and picked up ideas at a glance, but he didn't have the patience to work through a book that didn't interest him from the start. He even developed a technique to suit his impatience: whenever he picked up a new book, he turned to page 69, and if that page didn't impress him, he wouldn't read the book.[12] The uneasiness felt in Dreyfus's department at St Louis was evident throughout the ensuing decades. Renegade or not, Marshall really *could* be a sloppy and woolly researcher, and could be imprecise in his language. Yes, in the years to come he would threaten academia by taking up an essentially new subject,

---

[12] When I ask around, most people tell me that they reached their cruising speed of reading around third grade, and most people, if I pursue it, will admit that they've stuck with that reading speed from there on. Maybe not Marshall. Originally a product of Winnipeg's Alice Leone Mitchell School of Expression—which was all about reading aloud and for effect—he became a student of the Evelyn Wood Reading Dynamics, taught by his son Eric, and which was all about reading silently, for information, and with no expression at all.

The Evelyn Wood system was based on the idea that every person reads a word at the same rate, but a slow reader rereads words. Her method was to read every word by moving a finger or pointer, such as a pen, under each line of text at a steady pace. The pacing hand prevents rereading, resulting in an increase in comprehension and speed.

Most people, when reading a book, on a tiny yet perceptible level sub-vocalize the words they're reading in the back of their throats. You're probably doing it right now as you read these words ... feel it? It's not so much motion or vibration, but almost an invisible body awareness, the throat engaged at a tiny level. Speed-readers try to sever the link between the work on the page and this glottal, sensory (and emotional) engagement—removing its "effect" in a way that is a total repudiation of the aspect of taking in a text (in any medium) that mattered most to New Criticism—and to Marshall. Did any of these speed-reading tactics work? Marshall said that, in the end, they were only good for scanning data, and possibly for locating patterns, but not for the full enjoyment of reading.

but he *did* break good and important rules of scholarship and of scientific inquiry, as well perhaps as unnecessary and defensive ones. Thus, university staff always ran hot or cold on the man. Add to this Marshall's paranoid streak, imagining hostilities where none existed, and one sees that he was badly suited to the academic minefields of this realm. That he managed to remain in the university world as long as he did is, in itself, a feat of magic.

There might have been other reasons for the hostility McLuhan aroused. The distancing from his times, that divorce he felt from modernity, wedded to the hint of paranoia, left him quite outspokenly out of step, defensive, and intolerant. He was, truth be told, an illogical and fusty old vehicle for new ideas, and some people couldn't (and still can't) reconcile Marshall's appearance with what came out of his mouth. Perhaps if Marshall had looked like Bob Dylan, things might have turned out differently.

In January 1942 Corinne gave birth to a son, Thomas Eric, the first of six children. Marshall entered a new phase of life, and with it came a strange obsession—crystallized by fatherhood and by a fascination with the trappings of modern consumerist domesticity—with the comic strip character Dagwood Bumstead. Yes, it's as odd as it sounds, and no, he didn't build a shrine surrounded by yellowed newspaper clippings and a voodoo doll. But he *did* see that Dagwood typified all that was wrong with American males, and Dagwood became the jumping-off point of Marshall's 1951 book, *The Mechanical Bride*, a collection of analytical essays and often brilliant rants aimed at pieces of pop culture ephemera, and especially at how magazine advertisements sold the postwar dreams of everyday glamour and hygienic domesticity.

Marshall saw Dagwood as an emasculated drone who allowed industrial America to homogenize domestic life into three rectangular pussy-whipped panels a day, in colour on Sundays. It doesn't take a genius to establish that bumbling Dagwood Bumstead was Marshall's father, Herbert McLuhan, and Blondie the cryptodominatrix, Elsie. After growing up amid his mother's incessant hectoring and serial microabandonments (in the form of elocution tours), Marshall reached his verdict: Dagwood deserved all the humiliating daily punishments he received.

Marshall's Dagwood obsession foregrounded the fact that his critical writing only became truly fresh and alive when he fused formal academic knowledge with the observation of pop and media culture—when he used his words to span centuries and continents and knit them together. In an essay on jukeboxes, he wrote:

For tribal man, space was the uncontrollable mystery. For technological man it is time that occupies the same role. Time is still loaded with a thousand decisions and indecisions which terrify a society that has yielded so much of its autonomy to merely automatic processes and routines. The problem, therefore, is to control panic by "killing time" or by shredding it into "ragtime."

Even his worst detractor has to admit that McLuhan's attacks on consumer culture are both brilliant analyses—finding a critical language for a genre of texts that had never been subject to it before—and inspiringly livid, burbling cauldrons of raging snark. Marshall's soufflé only fell when he strayed from the modern era and its new vernaculars. I think he knew that quite soon. Oblivious or not, he quickly came to recognize that his arguments and language only truly connected with modern sensibility when he pushed the media button. Until he did that, he came across as a young old fart—which was fine if all he wanted to be was a generic academic. But that's not what he wanted. Elsie's son was going to shine. Even back in the glum, middle-American sameness of St. Louis, Marshall knew that a name, if it were to be made, would have to break the scholarly box, and that that break would somehow be connected with mass culture.

Marshall's Dagwood fixation also foregrounded his homophobia. There's really no other way to describe it. Blondie (embodying the industrial media complex) was pan-sifying American manhood. Marshall felt that homosexuality was "rampant in the age, the result of Blondie's emasculating Dagwood in front of Cookie and Alexander, their children. Such homosexuality was probably the chief threat to contemporary morality." Honestly, you can't make up stuff like this. Nor was Marshall a fan of postwar libera-tion, women's rights included. He described women as "con-stitutionally docile, uncritical, and routine loving." He would have lasted three minutes in a 2010 campus environ-ment. In so many ways he was a more than orthodox child of his era, and perhaps only his almost total silence in public about his reactionary view of politics and society, and gender, sin, and sexuality saved him from being marginal-ized in his own time.[13]

---

[13] Everyone likes to think that his or her own world view is the only true and reasonable world view. Marshall was no different in this regard. His prejudices reflect both his upbringing and his fervent embrace of Catholicism and its structure. It seems incongruent that the man could be ahead of the world in some ways and yet be retrograde in others. And I don't think it's even about being ahead of the times or behind the times. Marshall didn't really believe in time. He believed in eternity. Being alive on earth was but one phase of a larger process. His indifference to what we call "time" may have made him out of synch with society, but his disregard

Don't Mention the War

It was the middle of the Second World War, but his biographers allude to Marshall's engagement with it only in passing. His attitude to the war—to which he had seemed oblivious in Cambridge, and which came to the United States a month before his first child was born—reflects his cantankerous conservatism. The war's absence in his inner or outer world is striking. Biographers say that Marshall had zero sympathy for the Allies, and viewed the war as an updated exercise in modern technology homogenizing the process of killing. This is not to say that he was anti-war or a pacifist; he wasn't. He wouldn't take sides in the war—odd

---

for calendars also stripped him of the prejudices and assumptions that could limit his (or anybody's) thinking. I remember watching an old Cary Grant/Ingrid Bergman movie, *Notorious*, which is set in Miami during the Second World War. It starts with a party scene in which what happens, basically, is that Ingrid Bergman gets totally smashed and says, "Cary, we're both so incredibly drunk. Let's go out for a drive." And so they get out and go for a drive in Cary's convertible and a cop pulls them over and says (basically), "Okay, you two scallywags, be sure to drive more carefully because you're both pretty looped" ... and then they resume driving. And what struck me as weird during this whole sequence wasn't so much the booze and the driving as the fact that they were both *smoking*. Which is all to say that any of us are, at any given moment, guilty of countless physical and mental crimes yet to be invented and judged by future generations. And none of this excuses Marshall's behaviour, but yes, it does explain it a bit.

considering where and when he was living. How hard was it to say no to the Axis? Be that as it may, as a fully fit early-thirty-something Canadian citizen in robust good health, Marshall was primo combat beef, eligible to be drafted under U.S. law, his draftability confirmed by the glowing 1A classification he received in December 1943 from the St. Louis draft board. That same month, he also received his Cambridge D.Phil. for "The Place of Thomas Nashe in the Learning of His Time."

We look at the present through a rearview mirror.
We march backwards into the future.
M.M.

We shape our tools, and afterwards our tools shape us.
M.M.

Marooned

In the summer of 1943 Elsie was teaching drama in Detroit. To her surprise, she learned that across the St. Clair River, in Windsor, Ontario, was living the Canadian-born English painter and writer Wyndham Lewis, whom she knew Marshall much admired. Lewis, then sixty, had been a founder in 1913 of Vorticism[14] along with Ezra Pound, with whom the movement was also associated. Lewis's reputation as a leader of the avant-garde had taken a tumble as his writings became increasingly hostile to minorities, and it fell catastrophically in 1931 when he published a pro-Nazi study, *Hitler.* A retraction in 1939 did little to restore his respectability and—possibly an embarrassment to the British at home—Lewis returned to teach in wartime Canada to restore his battered finances. But it is obvious why McLuhan, about to begin his own explorations in the dynamics of culture, technology, and communication, was

---

[14] Vorticism was an art movement that—like futurism in Italy—responded to the modern world by drawing on the newly dynamic features of its industrial and social landscape, and—like cubism—by its faceted and fluid readings of natural physics and human psychology. Its literary expressions in particular were concerned with the fragmentation and force of language for its own sake. Much of the work was gathered into Lewis's revolutionary literary magazine, *BLAST,* in which textual freedoms, layout, graphics, and typographic experiments tried to visualize the message.

so excited by Lewis's inquiries and experiments in communication.

When McLuhan heard that Lewis was in Windsor, he and his friend and fellow Lewis fan Felix Giovanelli hopped on the train and raced to visit. The three men clicked, and Marshall returned to St. Louis eager to help his new, cash-poor friend earn money doing commissioned portraits. Wyndham arrived in St. Louis in February 1944 for a lucrative half-year visit. As repayment, he recommended that Marshall apply for an upcoming job as head of the English department at Windsor's Assumption College, a small Catholic school. It seemed like a terrific gig: the same pay, freedom from the St. Louis draft board, and a guaranteed reduced workload that would allow him to research and write. Perhaps he would rent a small house and let Junior run around the yard.

Mass transportation is doomed to failure in North America because a person's car is the only place where he can be alone and think.

M.M.

Directions to get home:

1: Start out going EAST on MARKET ST toward S 11TH ST.

0.4 mi.

2: Turn RIGHT onto S BROADWAY.

0.1 mi.

3: Turn LEFT onto WALNUT ST

 0.1 mi.

4: Turn RIGHT onto S MEMORIAL DR.

0.1 mi.

5: Merge onto I-55 N/I-70 E via the ramp on the LEFT toward ILLINOIS
   (Crossing into ILLINOIS)

19.3 mi.

6: Merge onto I-70 E via EXIT 20A toward INDIANAPOLIS (Crossing into
   INDIANA)

210.7 mi.

7: Merge onto I-465 S via EXIT 69 toward I-465 S/I-74 E.

28.7 mi

8: Merge onto I-69 N via EXIT 37 toward FT. WAYNE

96.6 mi.

9: Merge onto I-469 E/US-24 E via EXIT 96A

21.2 mi

10: Take the US-24 E exit, EXIT 21

0.3 mi.

11: Take the US-24 ramp.

0.0 mi.

12: Turn LEFT onto US-24 E (Crossing into OHIO)

84.9 mi.

13: Stay STRAIGHT to go onto ANTHONY WAYNE TRL/OH-25 N.

5.4 mi.

14: Merge onto I-75 N toward DETROIT (Crossing into MICHIGAN).

57.1 mi.

15: Take EXIT 47A toward M-3/CLARK AVE.

0.2 mi.

16: Stay STRAIGHT to go onto FISHER FWY W.

0.1 mi.

17: Turn RIGHT onto CLARK ST.

0.1 mi.

18: Turn LEFT onto FORT ST W/MI-3.

1.4 mi.

19: Turn RIGHT onto ROSA PARKS BLVD.

0.1 mi.

20: Stay STRAIGHT to go onto JEFFERSON AVE W.

0.7 mi.

21: Take the M-10 S ramp.

0.1 mi.

22: Turn SLIGHT RIGHT onto MI-10 S/JOHN C LODGE FWY.

0.3 mi.

23: MI-10 S/JOHN C LODGE FWY becomes JEFFERSON AVE W.

0.2 mi.

24: Turn RIGHT onto RANDOLPH ST.

0.0 mi.

25: Turn RIGHT onto DETROIT-WINDSOR TUNNEL (Portions toll)

0.1 mi.

26: Turn RIGHT to stay on DETROIT-WINDSOR TUNNEL (Crossing into CANADA)

1.0 mi.

27: Turn RIGHT0.1 mi.

28: Turn RIGHT onto PARK ST E.

0.1 mi.

29: Turn LEFT onto GOYEAU ST.

0.1 mi.

30: Turn RIGHT onto UNIVERSITY AVE E.

0.2 mi.

31: Turn SLIGHT RIGHT onto MCDOUGALL AVE.

0.0 mi.

32: End at Windsor, ON

Estimated Time: 9 hours 21 minutes Estimated Distance: 529.75 miles

Things Go Sideways

Marshall accepted the job, but it backfired: terrible students, classes taught in a coal-heated Quonset hut, and in the boredom sweepstakes, Windsor far eclipsed Toronto, Edmonton, Madison, or St. Louis. Marshall was marooned in a backwater with no direction or glamour or real passion, a crusty young man with his books, pipe, a young wife and son, and time whizzing by.

His relationship with Wyndham Lewis also deteriorated, and as happens with borderline low-grade paranoid schizo-phrenics, Wyndham wrote a list of wrongs Marshall had committed—an accretion of petty offences such as leaving Corinne in the car when visiting Lewis, being vain among the faculty in St. Louis, neglecting Corinne and Lewis once in Windsor—and then dismissed him as a friend. The sins were all sins of cluelessness. Marshall must have read the list and said, "Huh?" Merited or not, the axe came down. Eight years later, the men had a rapprochement, and they stayed in touch until Lewis's 1957 death. More importantly, in Lewis's 1948 book, *America and Cosmic Man*, Lewis wrote the words that became one of the clichés that defined McLuhan: "the earth has become one big village, with telephones laid on from one end to the other, and air transport, both speedy and safe."

In addition, Lewis the painter/writer gave McLuhan strong ideas about the way different styles of expression affect the senses in different registers. He also gave him the notion of being master of the vortex of change—the maelstrom of modernization—rather than being sucked in by it. Being a cultural observer was a survival strategy and an artistic strategy.

Space, Time, and the Machine

Another person who influenced McLuhan at this point was Sigfried Giedion, the Swiss architectural historian. Like McLuhan, Giedion—first in his famous *Space, Time & Architecture: The Growth of a New Tradition* (1941) and a little later in *Mechanization Takes Command* (1948), his analysis of how postwar mechanization would change culture—put forward a sort of unified theory of culture, and especially of the formation and transmission of new ideas from one generation to the next. He questioned the notions of authorship, copyright, style, sourcing, interpretation, bias, and audience, and saw cultural expressions in design, manufacture, and building as in some way deriving from a mass authorship, as if—like the internet today—the audience was writing its own play.

As with F.R. Leavis giving him permission to study popular culture, Giedion gave McLuhan intellectual permission to study not just novels, films, and poems, but *everything*, high or low, as a cultural artifact: litter, cathedrals, jet vapour trails, stacks of pancakes. As for an anthropologist, any artifact that might represent a culture was up for analysis. Giedion had aestheticized the world for Marshall, and the modern world now held for him the fascination of folk culture for an ethnologist. That is the point of observation he makes plain in the subtitle to his first full-length exploration of this new world around him: *The Folklore of Industrial Man.*

Was Marshall always simply shopping for intellectual authorities that would justify his (seemingly hard-wired) tendency to critique all levels of culture equally? Or was there an "Aha!" moment in Marshall's life when suddenly it all made sense? Andy Warhol (also a devout Catholic) once discussed driving across the United States in the early 1960s, saying how "pop" the landscape looked, with all its signs and advertising. He also mentioned that once you started seeing the world as pop, you could never go back to seeing it the way you did before. Perhaps Marshall's pop moment occurred during the shell shock of Cambridge versus Wisconsin, but if there was a specific moment, it remains unknown.

The Maelstrom

Marshall loved Edgar Allan Poe's 1841 short story, "A Descent into the Maelström," and I love him for introducing me to it. In Poe's tale, a young man sits at the top of a Norwegian mountain, beside the narrator, a seemingly old man of the sea. However, it turns out that the old man is, in fact, young—he had been prematurely aged by a storm a few years before that had led to a massive vortex in the ocean into which the man and his two brothers were swept. The younger brothers held on to large fragments of the ship and were swallowed. The narrator, though, noticed that heavy objects went down first; he held on to a barrel and managed to avoid his brothers' fate. It ends with the narrator knowing darn well that the younger person could care less about his story of survival.

As nearly all those who try to relate McLuhan to the internet have noted, this maelstrom is a marvellous metaphor for the way to keep one's head above water in a changing world. Rather than be sucked into a yawning, gaping mess, be nimble and analyze the broader scope of what's going on. Don't hang on to something that's going to drag you down. You may not like your environment, but don't allow it to overtake you or drown you.

www.youtube.com/watch?v=A7GvQdDQv8g

Marshall McLuhan on YouTube
Number of views: 59,521

231 ratings
☒ ☒ ☒ ☒ ☒
☒ Favorite   ☒ Share   ☒ Playlist   ☺ Flag

DFORCE1969
Reply: Before we all wax lyrically about the wonders of YouTube, look at the most popular vids: the medium is masturbation (literally and metaphorically).

KENRG
Reply: The predominant content, sure. I'm more interested in the power of the medium as whole, even if it's the less popular uses. I'm fairly certain McLuhan would agree, as he wrote his works in days of TV dominated by *The Beverly Hillbillies*, but still recognized the power of the medium to be much more important than that.

TOMNUNN07
Zengotita doesn't hold a candle to McLuhan in terms of media understanding and insight. McLuhan's rightful successor, who actually just died this past March, is Jean Baudrillard. Those serious about McLuhan should read Baudrillard's "Simulacra and Simulation."

HAUPPER
The medium is the mastodon.

CULTUSSTULTUS
Though we still use the new technology that mimics our nervous system, we dub, remix, re-edit, reframe, recontextualize all the footage to the point where we are now civilized in our jadedness and distance from the media. Remixes of 'Bus Uncle' and Xmen clips; reworking our perceptions of the theme to 'Mortal Kombat' whether by lip-synching or by posting our own recitals of it; animutation and parody to the nth degree all evidence this.

Fate Lobs a Softball

Marshall is, here in this book, the subject of a biography, but the ground against which he stands is the notion of "biography" itself. Before, say, 1990, biographies were how you really grew to know a person, but documentary filmmaking and the internet have closed the gap. Hardcover biographies still retain authority, though, probably because people are born, they do stuff, and then they die, and it's all a one-way trip—and this is a book, and like it or not, it has to be read in one direction and takes X amount of time to do so.

So within the borders of what you think a biography is and should be, you're hoping to learn new things about who Marshall was—and why he was—and with the good comes the bad. It's hard when you learn facts that don't fit the mould of preconceptions you began with. People are messy, accidents happen, coincidences occur, and most people are generally unprepared for, or don't see, coincidences when they happen. Marshall was a case of the right (though improbable) person more or less in the right place at the right time who didn't screw up when fate lobbed him a big, juicy softball. And who would have thought that Toronto, Canada, after the Second World War was the right time for anything, let alone big, juicy softballs? Canada then was sleeping and not even dreaming under the blanket of mother

119

England. The English considered the country to be something like aisles six through nine of a cosmic hardware store: lumber, fur, and metal products—with a grocery store sharing the same parking lot. What was Canada supposed to do with itself? What was Toronto supposed to be, other than a jumbo cashier's till and accountant's office? A place that created culture? A centre of something, anything? Toronto was for sleepwalkers, for the unambitious genetic residue of the Scottish, English, and Irish migrations, people happy to settle for a paycheque and relative freedom from change or chance.[15] The last person anyone would want in a place like this was Marshall McLuhan. By existing, in a way, he called into the spotlight the notion of Toronto's de facto nowhere status.

And yet ...

There *was* something going on in Toronto.

---

[15] My own family members who lived in Toronto in the 1950s remember it as being phantasmagorically boring and static—a bell jar inside which nothing would ever change and where all of life's decisions had been made for one beforehand. Ironically, when things really did start changing in the 1960s, decades of stasis had programmed these same family members to be horrified by the societal changes. The general consensus was that things were really good from about 1960 up to the November 1963 Kennedy assassination—and 1967 was kind of okay.

There was the growing awareness that media was itself something to be studied and that media was creating new laws and effects. Remember, there were no words to describe the emerging electronic world back then. Television was being born and by the early 1950s had begun its colossal and irreversible effect on Western life—an effect as profound as that of radio or the internet. The rise and rise of TV seemingly motivated Marshall to be more attuned to media and the daily world of information. Television was one more way of homogenizing and packetizing culture and, needless to say, Marshall loathed it but didn't want to be sucked into its vortex.[16]

Toronto was in a unique position to be objective about what was happening across both Lake Ontario and the Atlantic. It was a large modern city in a country unencumbered by overpowering political and religious orthodoxies like those found in Europe, the United States, and Asia. It offered a near-laboratory situation in which the effects of media could be empirically studied.

---

[16] In my observations, North Americans see history as a line on a graph always going up, headed *to* somewhere. Europeans tend to see history as a horizontal line merely heading from left to right. Marshall saw history as a line with a heavily downward slope. Just to clarify my position, I don't see history as a line—I see it as an ever-morphing volume with a shape rather than a direction.

The first to do so was Canadian scholar Harold Innis. In 1930 he wrote a book called *The Fur Trade in Canada: An Introduction to Canadian Economic History*. Innis claimed that the introduction of a new trade staple such as beaver pelts has a networking effect on society similar to introducing a new medium such as radio or film. Beaver pelts dictated the shape and scope of much of Canada—as did the completion of the national railway system. Intrigued by how a culture is made across a vastness like Canada's, Innis, up to his 1952 death, went on to look at the role of print and radio in connecting this huge, empty landscape. He stated that communications media are, in fact, technological extensions of our senses. Innis saw media as a way to shrink, expand, collapse, and reorder human notions of time and space.

McLuhan would shortly be working with Innis and others, because in early 1946 he received an offer to start teaching that fall at St. Michael's, the Catholic college at the University of Toronto.

Goodbye to Nowhere ...

In Toronto, Marshall would have all the psychic safety nets he wanted: a permanent home, his new family, Elsie living close by, a good job, and a strong church. At thirty-five, he wasn't what Elsie might consider a great success, but he was energetic and he was beginning to crank up his energy on the single trait that would ultimately bring him fame: pattern recognition.

Marshall was interested in the way modern culture homogenizes and renders modular all the things it touches—something as simple as time, for example. Before clocks, there was sunrise and sunset, but there was no way of standardizing time. With clocks, time was reduced to discrete hour chunks like hamburger patties, the same no matter where you go on the planet or, for that matter, outer space or even another galaxy. With music, there was the invention of the musical score, which turned religiously felt psalms into mere notes on a page. And of course, farm animals such as cows were homogenized into ... hamburger patties.

Marshall hated/abhorred/loathed the relentless commercialized standardization of the pre-scientific world, but in the immediate postwar years, progress through science was North America's dominant social agenda. Its effect on society was nascent and was clearly awaiting critical academic exploration.

... And Hello to Toronto!

Marshall, Corinne, and their three children (twin girls arrived at the end of 1945) moved to Toronto in 1946; the two parents stayed in the city the rest of their lives. Marshall was now seconds away from his work, as well as his church, where he took his daily break from mortal space-time and visited the celestial plane.

Marshall's college appointment had the added complexity of church politics thrown in. The college was one of many within the secular U of T system, but in 1946, St. Michael's students said prayers before class and needed permission from the college librarian to see books on the *Index Librorum Prohibitorum,* the Vatican's index of forbidden books. Even church apologist extraordinaire Marshall could feel the leaden hand of the clergy snuffing out some sparks from what was a good staff. But at the same time, because the college was Catholic, it brought in some amazing people, such as French philosophers Étienne Gilson and Jacques Maritain, and the new thoughts they expressed. Indeed, in the decade following the Second World War, English departments were actually thrilling places to be. An older set of students was challenging received wisdoms, and in Toronto, Northrop Frye—a central figure in Toronto's mid-century blossoming—had a sweeping view of culture that Marshall might have admired and drawn on. In fact, in a single city (Toronto—*what the hell?*) over a clear period of time, a small group of men revolutionized the way the world understands and uses communications.

Musician Glenn Gould, who, like Marshall, had a quirky brain and a corny sense of humour, was rewriting how music was made, ultimately renouncing public performance altogether in favour of music heard solely through electronic recording and radio that was a collage of found sound. (Marshall went on to become Gould's confidant for four-hour-long late-night conversations.) At the National Film Board, Norman McLaren was reinventing animation and time-based art, while a group of artists called Painters Eleven was exploring abstraction in painting. The great internationalist Lester Pearson won the Nobel Peace Prize, was soon to be prime minister, and was already setting the country's sights on a fanciful outlook in which the world started to talk as a family of man.[17]

When thinking about the University of Toronto and that era in history, one must consider both the bad and the good. It was adventurous, although it must be said that U of T's English department system was essentially a linked series of tree forts with a NO GIRLS ALLOWED sign hammered onto the

---

[17] Marshall believed that Canada had no identity of its own—and it was probably the freedom from overriding identity that helped create Toronto's emergence into a broader world. The biggest crystallization of this identity-via-nonidentity might be Expo 67's theme of a world without nations or, rather, man and his world. (Albeit, its pavilions were divvied up by nation.)

trunks below. Marshall may have generated a few enemies, but so did everybody else. Like so many academic settings, it was a bit of a Muppet Kremlin, and one of the good side effects of so many activities transpiring was that it created many cracks through which one might fall—which in some ways explains Marshall's ability to do all the things he did with a good degree of freedom. Here's a quick list of his connections at that point in time:

Friends:

Austere but benevolent **Father Louis Bondy**, who saw a spark in Marshall and hired him away from Windsor.

The roguish **Ted Carpenter**, U of T Department of Anthropology.

Harold Innis, U of T Department of Political Economy, the central hub of the country's intellectual world. More on him shortly.

Marshall's replacement in Windsor, **Hugh Kenner**. While not on U of T's faculty in the 1940s and early 1950s, Kenner was Marshall's confidant and co-conspirator and worked with him later at U of T.

Philosopher and iconoclast **George Grant**. Like Marshall, Grant was leery of technology, with thinking rooted in Christianity. Not a U of T prof but made a big footprint there.

Frequent visiting French philosopher **Étienne Gilson**, who in today's world might only wear black turtleneck sweaters; he saw brilliant but often alarming iconoclastic ideas in Marshall.

Enemies:

Central casting fussbudget bachelor **A.S.P. Woodhouse**, head of University College English department. He hated, hated, *hated* Marshall and saw in him the New Criticism and the end of the dynasty he'd been running for ages.

Most of Marshall's colleagues. They viewed him as a nutbar with weirdly few social skills, and interpreted his bombastic, combative demeanour as a threat and his indifference to standard teaching tasks as an insult.

Literary critic **Northrop Frye**, a faculty member of another U of T college, Victoria College. The two men disliked each other and had a feud that livened up the campus. One suspects that people on both sides stoked the flames for entertainment value.

Jehoshaphat!

In 1947 a third daughter was born to Marshall and Corinne. Marshall was learning that families are expensive. He was approaching forty. He was beginning to experience frustration with being financially and academically ghettoized in a Catholic college. If he was going to be Elsie's golden boy, he was going to have to do something large quite soon, and he knew one could be golden only outside of the University of Toronto's English department.

In 1948 Marshall visited Washington, D.C., with his friend Hugh Kenner. They went to see Ezra Pound, an Idaho-born American poet, critic, and intellectual, and a major figure of the modernist movement in the first half of the twentieth century. Kenner went on to become the preeminent biographer of and scholar on Pound as a result of this meeting.

In 1939 Pound, a passionate supporter of Mussolini, had moved to Italy, becoming a leading Axis propagandist on Italian radio. In 1943 he was indicted for treason by the U.S. government and brought back to the United States. To preclude the country from executing one of its greatest writers, Pound was declared incompetent to face trial and was placed in St. Elizabeth's Hospital in Washington, D.C., where he remained for twelve years, from 1946 to 1958. He died in 1972.

In Pound, Marshall saw for himself the protons and neutrons at the core of early twentieth-century modernist literature—the intelligence, the craziness, and the crackling oddness of it all—and his fandom was of the rock star mould. Little is known of the relationship between the two men, other than that it was mostly one way, from Marshall's side. Pound had little use for Marshall's ideas and articles that were sent along to his Washington, D.C., madhouse.

If nothing else, the doggedness with which Marshall courted both Pound and Wyndham Lewis reveals the depth of his respect for the modernist guillotining of nineteenth-century literature and an indication, perhaps, of how much he wished he could have been there to experience that moment.

In the same vein, in 1950 Marshall became obsessed with James Joyce's novel *Finnegans Wake* (1939), a free-association spree of multilingual puns and portmanteau words (words melted together to create new words). Puns, you say? Catnip for Marshall, whose zest for punning was a distinct brain pathology. Once Marshall's fervour for the book was established, he enjoyed using a rich Oirish brogue to read passages from the book to friends and students.

Jehoshaphat, what doom is there here!

The novel's writing style, its literary allusions, its dream associations, and its dismissal of conventions of plot and character construction have largely prevented it from being read by the general public, a factor that made it even more tantalizing to Marshall. He saw the book as a potential Rosetta stone—a unified theory of culture that could prescribe the healthiest balance between hearing the world and seeing the world. The book also represented to Marshall the twentieth-century fall of man from grace into a world in which a healthy mental ecosystem is utterly changed in a harmful way by the advent of electronic media and a disruption of the balance of senses used in daily life.

The book remained a touchstone for almost all his future work.

> The simplification of anything is always sensational.
> G.K. Chesterton

Publishing the *Bride*

And so, in Toronto, Marshall began in force his program of mapping himself onto mass culture. In 1951 he published *The Mechanical Bride*. The title refers to the famous 1912 work by artist Marcel Duchamp called *The Bride Stripped Bare by Her Bachelors, Even*, a huge two-panel glass sculpture on the theme of the eroticization of the machine. When

Marshall wrote the book, the sculpture was possibly the best-known avant-garde work of art in the twentieth century, second only to Duchamp's earlier urinal sculpture. For Marshall, the title of his book was a reflection on the new status of the machine and how it is sold—the mechanical bride is the car as a love object in a world in which we have been seduced by and have married mechanization.

The book was a compilation of new and previously published rants and sharpened darts aimed at secular Western media culture, a medieval Catholic curse on Hollywood and Madison Avenue. It was a large hardcover, not unlike a Dr. Seuss–sized book in terms of touch and feel. Most of the rants appeared opposite the ads that inspired them, and there was no particular order to the essays. As with most of Marshall's books, he employed a mosaic text format that allowed the reader to dip in and out of the book at whim, as though looking at a website.

The Mechanical Bride was Dagwood's day in the sun— that is, a big black sun that wanted Dagwood dead. Today the book feels alternately hokey, prescient, quippy, brilliant, sophomoric, and delirious. It inhabits a media world as might be experienced by Salinger's Holden Caulfield, and like Caulfield, Marshall finds hypocrisy and hyperbole everywhere. Nearly six decades after the book's publication, everybody in Western society is a critic, and everybody has theories about TV, film, and advertising. What makes *The Mechanical Bride* magic is that McLuhan was arguably the first person on earth to be a metacritic. Some of his thrusts are clunky, but they represent the first modernist moment when the beak pokes through the eggshell. The book represents a sort of birth.

At first, only a few hundred copies of *The Mechanical Bride* sold, though in the decades since, many reprints have emerged. The *Bride's* publication also marked the last point in McLuhan's career when he focused on the physical products of mass society. But the *Bride*, in its fascination with how words and images are melted together to sell commodities, starts to propose new ways to look at styles of communication and their subliminal messages. From this point on, McLuhan's work moves progressively, and quickly, from the material culture of the technological world to its mass media and the emerging electronic dimension they now work within. In the same way, *The Mechanical Bride* marks both the end of McLuhan's focus on content and the beginning of his movement away from what was being said to *how* it was being said; to the ways in which content is put forth into the world, both through type and the phonetic alphabet (*The Gutenberg Galaxy*, 1962) and on the TV tube (*Understanding Media*, 1964).

A commercial society whose members are essentially ascetic and indifferent to social
ritual has to be provided with blueprints and specifications
for evoking the right tone for every occasion.
M.M.

Ads are the cave art of the twentieth century.
M.M.

Advertising is an environmental striptease for a world of abundance.
M.M.

The Mechanical Bride: Folklore of Industrial Man[18]

MCLUHAN, Herbert Marshall.
Bookseller location: London, England
Bookseller Rating: 4-star rating
Price: US$ 3,450.00

Book Description:
New York: Vanguard Press
1951
Quarto, 157pp.

A first edition of McLuhan's first book, it inaugurated of one of the most eccentric and intellectual careers of his time, whose insights have become, in some instances, ill-digested commonplaces or still-radical assessments of a technological and media culture.

A very good or better copy in publisher's textured glossy paper-covered boards and a less than very good example of the publisher's illustrated dust jacket.

Inscribed by McLuhan, "Cordial regards to Wyndham Lewis from Marshall McLuhan."

McLuhan and Lewis were close friends during the forties and fifties, and McLuhan frequently cites Lewis's work in his own, normally as a neglected voice of sanity whose work will repay examination, as he does in the present work. McLuhan's notion of the "global village" is found pre-figured in a remark of Lewis's in *America and Cosmic Man* (1948). Lewis was among the most sophisticated of modernist writers and authors, and his thoughtful social commentary remains rather marginal due to coruscations

---

[18] Online book sales shown in these pages are culled from www.abebooks.com, with enough information deleted to protect the identity of both buyer and seller.

of what have consistently been dismissed as reactionary ravings. T.S. Eliot, himself no stranger to similar criticism (and neither of them completely unfairly so criticized), called Lewis, "the most fascinating personality of our time," and "the only one among my contemporaries to create a new, and original, prose style." Though British, Lewis was born in Canada, lived there in childhood and returned during the Second World War, making the present a Canadian association copy of the first rank.

Bookseller Inventory # 11775NK

Quantity: 1

Add Book to Shopping Basket?

Yelling Across a Broad Land

Harold Adams Innis (he of *The Fur Trade in Canada*) pioneered the study of media and was a giant's shoulder on which Marshall was able to stand. Innis was a big deal. In 1946 he was elected president of the Royal Society of Canada, the country's senior body of scientists and scholars. In 1947 he was appointed the University of Toronto's dean of graduate studies. He thought highly of McLuhan's ideas—he placed *The Mechanical Bride* on his students' reading lists—and the fact that both men were Canadian and ended up literally writing the books on media theory together is more than coincidence. Their ability to contemplate wide distances with no overriding imperialist agenda gave both men a sense of intellectual freedom, as it did with other minds working in Toronto at the same time. As a bonus, for Marshall to have someone high up on the U of T food chain helping him was a bit of a raspberry at his in-house naysayers.

Innis's and McLuhan's ideas about electronic media both overlapped and had differences. Innis was interested in the way various media collapse (or reconfigure) time and space; McLuhan focused on the way media shift the degree to which a society favours the eye or the ear. Innis's last book, *The Bias of Communication* (1951), looks at the impact of literacy and its technologies on civilization. McLuhan carried the torch forward, exploring communications far more radically in his 1962 book, *The Gutenberg Galaxy*.

But above all, McLuhan built on Innis's idea that, in studying communications media, technological form matters more than content. Biographer Paul Heyer wrote that Innis's concept of the "bias" of a particular medium of communication can be seen as a "less flamboyant precursor to Marshall's legendary phrase 'the medium is the message.'" If Innis hadn't died of prostate cancer in 1952, who knows what might have come from further collisions of his mind with McLuhan's?

Innis certainly would have been fascinated by (and felt validated by) the impact of TV and radio in Quebec in the 1950s and 1960s, the ways in which media created the Quiet Revolution. Over a decade, millions of Québécois broke free from the grip of the Church and the yoke of the closest thing to Stalin ever created in North America, Maurice Duplessis, creator of the Great Darkness. Within a decade, Quebec became electrically wired and highly secular. It also became politically self-aware, and in the 1970s began pushing the boundaries of how far a distinct society could coexist within a larger democratic union.

Disinhibited!

Marshall was a terrific professor, and it takes little energy to imagine him in his prime, burying students in cascades of ideas—not infrequently, ideas he generated on the spot. As time went on, Marshall's classes were packed and over-flowing. Marshall wasn't an exhibitionist. Rather, he had what you might call a sort of low-grade disinhibitory condition in which certain modes of being and thinking could only take place as long as there was an audience present. He found it much more preferable to do his thinking in real time, out loud, with an audience or a classroom as his cata-lyst. *Conversation* is what he called it.[19]

After a while, students learned that if they approached Marshall's classes like other classes, they were doomed to confusion and bafflement. Instead, the thing to do was simply to show up and listen to the words and feel the sparks the words ignited within their craniums. It's not as if there was a formal agenda and one either learned it or not. The key to *getting* the man seemed to be to open your mind—relax it a touch—and then expose yourself to his thoughts.

---

[19] This mild disinhibitory condition also helps account for his preference, especially later in life, to create books unless collaborating with at least one other person.

You might not agree with them, you might not even fully understand them (indeed, some of them might not be understandable), but your own ideas would be ignited by their weirdly bureaucratic metre and their hyperprecision.

His Tipping Point

In 1952 Marshall's sixth and final child was born, a boy. Marshall was also made a full professor at U of T. During this period, he became obsessed with secret societies that he believed were colluding to keep him from being more successful than he was and blackballing him from academic publications. This belief was scotched when, in 1953, Marshall received a grant from the Behavioral Sciences division of the Ford Foundation. Marshall and his intellectual sparring partner, the raunchy, ribald anthropologist Edmund (Ted) Carpenter, were given $44,250—a whopping sum for the time.

Wait—an anthropologist working with an English professor? Yes. Their mission was to create a series of interdisciplinary communications seminars. These days, such seminars occur daily in community colleges across the planet, but in 1953 the notion of interdisciplinary studies was racy and suspect. Postwar America was about society renegotiating its relationship with technology. Specialization was king. Why hybridize thought? Why widen focuses when a narrowing was called for?

McLuhan and Carpenter's intent was to build on Innis's notion of how a medium reshapes the environment in which it operates. As stated earlier, TV was on the ascent and people could feel change crackling in the air, but there were no words or theories to describe or analyze this sense of change. The Ford Foundation wanted to develop new means of defining a new world; Marshall's timing was ideal.

As interdisciplinary partners, Marshall chose U of T economics professor Tom Easterbrook (his Winnipeg friend with whom he had visited England), psychology professor Carl Williams, and an architecture professor and theorist of urban networks named Jacqueline Tyrwhitt—a friend of Sigfried Giedion and a rare female given admittance into Marshall's academic universe.[20]

The seminars were an instant hit; this is when Marshall started becoming the Super-Marshall of the 1960s. He had an eager audience, excellent minds to bounce ideas around with. The university was beginning to realize that something was happening. Staff from other faculties began attending the seminars. Innis's work was examined and brought back

---

[20] Of 185 authors cited in *The Gutenberg Galaxy*, three are women, more an indication of the era than anything else.

to life, and Marshall and other seminar members explored new ideas on how different media affect our senses in different ways. Most important was Marshall's focus on how various media shift our brains' focus between visual and acoustic space—this was the key that turned the engine of his 1962 hit, *The Gutenberg Galaxy*.

What gave the Ford seminars their buzz was that discoveries began triggering new discoveries. Suddenly, the entire culture (and all cultures) could be conceived of as a technology: TV, radio, and film, as well as all forms of printed and typeset information—maps, Bibles, language, scripts—everything. Voilà! There, in Toronto in 1953, a nascent media language emerged, later to be called the Toronto School of Communication Theory, triggered by the electronic tipping point caused by the introduction of TV. The world was collectively experiencing a wide-scale psychic rupture—as forceful as the one it would later experience with the arrival of the internet.[21]

The seminars marked a key departure for Marshall, too. Rather than focusing on the effects of English literature on the individual reader, he became more interested in technology and *its* effects on the individual—as had been

---

[21] One of the most potent and happy memories of many people born before 1950 is the arrival of the first TV set into the house.

demanded by the New Criticism. In some ways, Marshall simply applied the premises of the New Criticism to *everything*. Suddenly, within the U of T English faculty, there was this relative newcomer who was becoming well known (not yet famous; that would happen in 1962), who seemingly didn't care as much about English as he once did. To add to the aggravation of the Lit program's staff, they had a niggling sense that there was a good chance this McLuhan guy might not only be right in what he was saying, but might also be spelling out a future path for study that the rest of us weren't trained to walk on.

Marshall was also encountering a response that would tail him the rest of his life: the incorrect belief that he liked the new world he was describing. In fact, he didn't ascribe any moral or value dimensions to it at all—he simply kept on pointing out the effects of new media on the individual. And what makes him fresh and relevant now is the fact that (unlike so much other new thinking of the time) he always *did* focus on the individual in society, rather than on the mass of society as an entity unto itself. It was Marshall's embrace of the individual—a poetic and artistic, highly humane embrace—that has allowed the reader (then and now) to enter his universe. There are, perhaps, no practical political, religious, or financial applications to Marshall's work. It could even be argued that it should be seen as a rarefied artifact unto itself, an intricate and fantastically ornate artwork that creates its own language and then writes poetry with it. And what would be wrong with that? Art is art. And an artist, according to Marshall, is someone on the frontiers of perception, who looks at information overload with the goal of pattern recognition, to see things before anyone else.

Major *Explorations*

Along with the seminars, Marshall McLuhan and Ted Carpenter started a journal called *Explorations*, printing six editions over two years.[22] *Explorations'* mandate was to reflect the discoveries of the Ford seminars and act as a house organ for Marshall and his coterie to air their new ideas in public. It was a glorious stew of diamonds and rhinestones and Fabergé eggs and *merde*, and even today its issues drip with still-fresh ideas as simple as: What is time? What is the

---

[22] *Explorations'* energy reminds me of *Wired* magazine's energy in the early 1990s, when McLuhan was listed on its masthead as a "Patron Saint." One thing I remember about *Wired* at this time is that everybody was carping about how unreadable the magazine looked: *They're mixing fonts. Text changes size throughout the article. The colours are hurting my eyes.* By 1995, when I worked for a while at *Wired*, the typography debate had died down, and when I look back on those layouts now, they're about as tame-looking as any spread in current issues of *Mademoiselle*.

self? What is the media world, and how is it changing us? *Explorations* became Marshall's calling card throughout the world. It gave him intellectual confidence and a wider base for his inquiries and probes. And its existence, as with most of what Marshall did, alarmed those colleagues still bunkered in specialized technology-powered Cold War bunkers.

> It requires a very unusual mind to undertake the analysis of the obvious.
> Alfred North Whitehead

Explorations

CARPENTER, Edmund; MCLUHAN, Marshall [editors]
Bookseller location: Chicago, Ill.
Bookseller Rating: 4-star rating
Price: US$ 475.00

Book Description: Explorations, Toronto
1953
Wrappers. Book Condition: Very Good
First Edition; 8 volumes

A complete set of this fantastic magazine issued from 1953–1959.
McLuhan was an associate editor of the first nine issues and a co-editor for
the final two issues. Issues contain major works by McLuhan as well as
work by D.T. Suzuki, Northrop Frye, G. Legman, David Riesman, Jorge Luis
Borges, Ralph Maud and many others.

The magazine continued in different formats and sizes after this, but these
initial eight editions are considered seminal to McLuhan's media discoveries.

Issue 4 is worn about edges and spine but all other issues are very good to
near fine condition, scarce thus.

Bookseller Inventory # 22885

Quantity: 1

Add Book to Shopping Basket?

Probes

Flush with intellectual vim from his seminars and his magazine, Marshall began to create what he called *probes*, a conversational format in which ideas were thrown out into a collective arena without moral judgment and allowed to battle it out, with the goal of generating new ideas. By now, the absence of a moral stance or judgment was a deliberate strategy. Morality often impedes free thinking. Moral indignation is a salve for people unable or unwilling to try to understand. Again the maelstrom: understand your world and detach from it, or be drowned by it. The world is understandable; too much information makes it feel like it isn't. Look for patterns. Invert your biases. Debate the other side's point of view—anything except take it for what it first appears to be. Marshall said, "All ignorance is motivated." A starving Ethiopian might disagree, but Marshall's thrust is that a world needs to be created where, if nothing else, everyone from starving Ethiopians to the king of Sweden feels that they have hope, a set of tools, and a sense of empowerment to go about understanding their world and changing it if they can.

The biggest intellectual leap during this era was Marshall's ever more precise definition of what we call *space*. In our culture, space is something one sees in front of one's eyes. We are largely trained not to think of soundscapes or odourscapes or any other scapes. Sight rules. But this dominance is a pretty recent thing. Marshall's thinking was that up until the marriage of the phonetic alphabet, paper, and the printing press, people perceived the world primarily by sound, with vision a distant second. This seems counterintuitive (obviously we see the world all day every day), yet Marshall wasn't simply discussing the way we perceive volume but rather the way those volumes are *experienced*. That's a finicky but necessary difference to establish; hearing was vastly more important five hundred years ago than it is today.

This notion of how the body senses the universe—the phenomenology of space—brings us back to the question of autism. Facts: Marshall hated being touched or jostled; he hated abrupt noises or extraneous sounds; he loved words and the repetition of words and punning. In the 1960s he began to resent it when people asked him how he was feeling—a sentiment he ascribed to being overbombarded with information. But again, much of Marshall's behaviour seems to place him on the mild end of the autistic spectrum; it's not difficult to suppose that a man so sensorially skewed might be interested in investigating this skewedness. Marshall's lifelong investigations can, in part, be framed as witting or unwitting attempts to make peace with the brain and body he was born with.

Life on Earth

The late 1950s were probably the most intellectually electric period of Marshall's life. New ideas crackled around his head like Tesla waves. Society was absorbing too much technology too quickly, and he knew it. Did he like this? No! He hated, loathed, abhorred it. There was a small window in the late 1950s when he had a drop of hope that the world might become a better place with new technology—but that hope quickly died with the decade. As of the 1960s, Marshall viewed the mortal world as a lost cause because of both pollution and technology, and he pined for another era, a different time stream, a different universe—*anything* different from booming North America's guns-and-butter praxis. How the man ever came to be perceived as technology's cheerleader is a mystery. Not that any of this stopped McLuhan on his quest for ideas.

Right Place, Right Time

Marshall's grasp of new media came about to a large extent because: (1) He did his doctoral thesis on the obscure sixteenth-century pamphleteer Thomas Nashe; (2) His mother made him learn to elocute; (3) His brain was wired in an unusual way; (4) He had two arteries, not one, feeding blood to his brain; (5) He found a religion; (6) He grew up in the Canadian Prairies; (7) He was obsessed with Dagwood Bumstead; (8) He was an expert on James Joyce. To these and many other factors, add: (9) He received a 1959 commission to prepare a syllabus for American grade eleven students, a course of study on the effects of newly emerging electronic media—not their content but, rather, their grammar and their *mutational powers*. It, and the $15,000 associated with it, came from the National Association of Educational Broadcasters and the U.S. Office of Education. This offer didn't come totally out of the blue. *Explorations* had a solid readership, and word about McLuhan was leaking out. The dike had yet to burst, but it was certainly leaking. The NAEB's money allowed Marshall to take a one-year sabbatical and hire a research assistant and a full-time secretary, Margaret Stewart.

Feeding on ideas and energy from both the Ford seminars and *Explorations*, the NAEB report gave Marshall a necessary lens through which he could focus his all-over-the-map ideas. On a subliminal level, they worked toward creating a possible unified theory of culture. Heady stuff!

And by focusing on grade eleven students, Marshall was forced to study the *terra incognita* of the post-industrial brainscape; no need to deprogram fogey old brains—he could harvest dewy young TV-moulded brains. And by studying the *effects* of media, he was also forced to focus on the physical effects of TV, the radio, and the telephone. This was a crucial step in linking scientific effects to artistic effects. Anybody who's ever been on a telephone conference call knows how it sucks all the joy, life, and oxygen out of the room. Anyone who's ever taken a nap with a TV or radio on in the background knows how it temporarily sedates certain kinds of thought processes.

Marshall thought of his media discoveries as so vital and transformative that he chose to work with an array of experts from all disciplines, in particular, engineers. He believed that scientific processes dictate how a medium becomes a message. Television cathode ray tubes project directly onto the retina. Light bounces off a painting. Electric light projects onto the retina but contains no information. And so on. Oddly, aside from a fervent belief later in his life about the two lobes of the brain and how they accomplished what they each regulated, Marshall never delved too much into neuroanatomy. This was a generation and a half before diagnoses such as depression or Asperger syndrome became commonly understood. It was the era of the frontal lobotomy, and in that pre-MRI world, the brain was still an enigmatic beige pudding. One wonders what Marshall would have made of, say, Prozac, Wellbutrin, Abilify, or Paxil. But because there was no real mapping of the specific functions of each brain cortex or node or region, the only way inside the brain circa 1958 was the imagination. To this end, Marshall began creating sets of rules and laws for describing media and their effects—terms like *hot* and *cool, low definition* and *high definition.* The roots of most of Marshall's future pronouncements on the effects of media were present in the NAEB report.

Marshall's first draft was completed in June 1960, and a final document entitled *Report on Project in Understanding New Media* was published later that year. Oh, to have been a fly on the wall when the NAEB opened the report and gave it a read—the dropped jaws! The baffled expressions! The NAEB did, to its credit, recognize brilliance in the report, but its total absence of connection to the life and mind of a grade eleven student made it unusable. Its confusing charts, its heaps of esoterica, all glued together by Marshall's dense, metaphor-rich style of writing alienated all but the most determined reader.

Producing the book came with a price. The two years spent making it were arguably the most exploration-rich of Marshall's life. But the stress on his brain took a toll. In early 1960 he suffered a stroke so severe that a priest was called in for last rites. Marshall survived but was forced to rest by his doctor. The medical event was kept under wraps, and in the fall of 1961, Marshall resumed teaching, with only a few people close to him aware of the intellectual and physical journey he'd been on.

A Silent Death

Elsie had also had a stroke—in 1956—an event that left her unable to speak, and that was nearly identical to the stroke that would finally silence Marshall in 1979. Elsie died in July 1961. Herbert would die in 1966.

Marshall, for all his spleen toward American manhood (he once labelled them "Sixty Million Mama's Boys"), was a mama's boy. Elsie's DNA and nurturing had been the most powerful influences in his life. He expressed his love and devotion for her in a Marshall kind of way: he took the bus to the hospital and, while she lay in bed, sat and read her detective stories.

Let the Sixties Begin!

The narcotic stasis of the Cold War era was beginning to wear off. It was the final few hours of a time when men still wore hats. Women celebrated pregnancies with cocktails. Everyone smoked. Legally sanctioned apartheid existed in the United States. Television was only a decade old, only then shifting to the novelty of colour—with peacocks and rainbows as network symbols—and had yet to mould society by widening access to information and overcoming the divide between literate and non-literate, high culture and low. Soon to be on the menu: hippies, lunar missions, the Chinese People's Revolution, Vietnam, African decolonization, Black Panthers, LSD, the Summer of '68, the pill ... and Marshall.

The month of Elsie's death, in July 1961, Marshall had begun assembling a wide array of materials he'd written over the previous decade. He was going to make them into a book, and this can't have been a coincidence. Marshall was going to make Elsie proud, and this book would be his love letter to her memory. *The Mechanical Bride* had been published a decade before, and if Marshall was going to become renowned and worthy of being Elsie's son, it certainly wouldn't be by publishing articles in small-circulation literary journals and futzing about with U of T English department micropolitics. In what was possibly the most focused three months of his life, Marshall cobbled together *The Gutenberg Galaxy*. It was published in 1962 and remains one of the most brilliant books on books and the effects of print and reading ever written.

... escape
... control

Immediate Meshes Hugest
Immediate Themes Gushes
Mesdames Eightieth Muse
Mesdames Eightieth Emus
Aesthete Sighed Mummies
Sheathes Gummed Itemise
Sheathe Edgiest Mummies
Sheathe Demise Gummiest
Hesitates Hedge Mummies
Atheise Meshed Gummiest
Athetise Hedges Mummies
Hesitate Hedges Mummies
Sesame Summed Eightieth
Haughtiest Seemed Mimes
Geishas Teethed Mummies
Messaged Tithe Hues Mime
Sheathed Siege Mime Smut
Sheathed Siege Mime Must
Sheathed Siege Time Mums
Sheathed Siege Emit Mums
Sheathed Siege Mite Mums
Sheathed Siege Item Mums
Sheathed Segue Mime Mist
Sheathed Egis Mime Mutes
Sheathed Egis Mimes Mute
Sheathed Guise Mime Stem
Sheathed Gems Mime Suite
Sheathed Guess Mime Time
Sheathed Guess Mime Emit
Sheathed Guess Mime Mite
Sheathed Guess Mime Item
Sheathed Guest Mime Semi

Headiest Siege Them Mums
Headiest Theme Egis Mums
Headiest Theme Semi Smug
Headiest Theme Semi Gums
Headiest Theme Semi Mugs
Headiest These Mime Smug
Headiest These Mime Gums
Headiest These Mime Mugs
Headiest Sheet Mime Smug
Headiest Sheet Mime Gums
Headiest Sheet Mime Mugs
Headiest Thee Mimes Smug
Headiest Thee Mimes Gums
Headiest Thee Mimes Mugs
Headiest Seem Eight Mums
Headiest Seem Mime Thugs
Headiest Seem Mimes Thug
Headiest Seem Muse Might
Headiest Seem Emus Might
Headiest Seems Mime Thug
Headiest Meets Mime Hugs
Headiest Meets Mime Gush
Headiest Metes Mime Hugs
Headiest Metes Mime Gush
Headiest Teems Mime Hugs
Headiest Teems Mime Gush
Headiest Meet Mimes Hugs
Headiest Meet Mimes Gush
Headiest Mete Mimes Hugs
Headiest Mete Mimes Gush
Headiest Teem Mimes Hugs
Headiest Teem Mimes Gush

Headiest Huge Mime Stems
Headiest Huge Mimes Stem
Headiest Guess Them Mime
Headiest Guest Hems Mime
Headiest Guest Mesh Mime
Atheised Siege Them Mums
Atheised Theme Egis Mums
Atheised Theme Semi Smug
Atheised Theme Semi Gums
Atheised Theme Semi Mugs
Atheised This Mime Smug
Atheised These Mime Gums
Atheised These Mime Mugs
Atheised Sheet Mime Smug
Atheised Sheet Mime Gums
Atheised Sheet Mime Mugs
Atheised Thee Mimes Smug
Atheised Thee Mimes Gums
Atheised Thee Mimes Mugs
Atheised Seem Eight Mums
Atheised Seem Mime Thugs
Atheised Seem Mimes Thug
Atheised Seem Muse Might
Atheised Seem Emus Might
Atheised Seems Mime Thug
Atheised Meets Mime Hugs
Atheised Meets Mime Gush
Atheised Metes Mime Hugs
Atheised Metes Mime Gush
Atheised Teems Mime Hugs
Atheised Teems Mime Gush
Atheised Meet Mimes Hugs

Atheised Meet Mimes Gush
Atheised Mete Mimes Hugs
Atheised Mete Mimes Gush
Atheised Teem Mimes Hugs
Atheised Teem Mimes Gush
Atheised Huge Mime Stems
Atheised Huge Mimes Stem
Atheised Guess Them Mime
Atheised Guest Hems Mime
Atheised Guest Mesh Mime
Hesitated Gees Mime Hums
Hesitated Gees Mime Mush
Hesitated Seem Mime Hugs
Hesitated Seem Mime Gush
Hesitated Huge Mime Mess
Hesitated Gems Hues Mime
Headsets Eight Mime Muse
Headsets Eight Mime Emus
Headsets Huge Mime Times
Headsets Huge Mime Smite
Headsets Huge Mime Emits
Headsets Huge Mime Items
Headsets Huge Mime Mites
Headsets Huge Mimes Time
Headsets Huge Mimes Emit
Headsets Huge Mimes Mite
Headsets Huge Mimes Item
Headsets Guise Them Mime
Headset Segue Mime Smith
Headset Eights Mime Muse
Headset Eights Mime Emus
Headset Eight Mime Muses
Medium The Message The Is

The Gutenberg Galaxy: The Making of Typographic Man

MCLUHAN, Herbert Marshall.
Bookseller location: Flagstaff, AZ, USA
Bookseller Rating: 4-star rating
Price: US$ 380.25

Book Description:
University of Toronto Press
1962
First edition; Hardcover.
Dust Jacket Included.
294 pages; few short tears, creased

Bookseller Inventory # 188175NR

Quantity: 1

Add Book to Shopping Basket?

The politician will be only too happy to abdicate in favor of his image, because the image will be so much more powerful than he will ever be.
M.M.

When our identity is in danger, we feel certain that we have a mandate for war. The old image must be recovered at any cost.
M.M.

Still Life with Airport

You are in an airport and the year is 1962. Women around you are dressed nicely. You are wearing a hat. You are a fifty-two-year-old man eating roast beef in an airport restaurant, and the roast beef you are eating is marbled with globs of fat shaped like American states and counties. The air is silky blue with cigarette smoke. There are no black people around you. You are reading newspaper articles about birth control pills and about art being made in New York that uses comic strips and magazine ads as its creative nucleus. The ice in your bourbon is almost entirely melted. Your flight is announced and you go to your gate. You get into your seat, 3A, and the guy seated beside you pinches the stewardess's butt. She giggles.

You cross a continent.

The car that picks you up at the other end is a machine that pumps large clouds of leaded blue smoke into the air while it idles. All the other cars around you are doing the same thing. None of these cars have seat belts. The sky is brown.

A woman on the sidewalk takes a pill. Pills of all sorts seem so common: amphetamines for people trying to lose weight, elephant-pill barbiturates for those in need of sleep. But your brain is calm. Your brain feels like a cathedral made of brown stone, light beaming in through stained-glass windows. You are witnessing the world, but you are not being affected by it. You are driven to a skyscraper where rich men are paying you thousands of dollars to say pretty much whatever passes through your mind.

Kaboom!

The 1962 reviews of *The Gutenberg Galaxy* were ecstatic. It won Canada's Governor General's Award for Nonfiction. It was widely reviewed and widely regarded as brilliant. Its idiosyncratic writing style, mixed with its tendency to repeat itself, chilled a few critics, while others found swaths of the book simply nuts. Marshall became the kid with an intellectual peanut allergy who alerts us to a tainted world. The book posits so many ideas—it moves toward a sense of longing for some new, yet-to be invented mode of being. It states over and over again that it abhors the desacralized present world, where God is absent and only our basest motives are facilitated. It attributes only homogenizing effects to most scientific advances. It's obvious Marshall can't stand the mortal world, and at various times he comes across as arrogant, charming, funny, boring, inflammatory, clueless, stoked, godlike, and full of horseshit—but you keep on reading. Curiously, after making our way through page after page of Marshall's disdain for the world, on page 135 of the Canadian paperback edition, we find, like a message in a bottle, one line that provides hope: "Far from belittling the Gutenberg mechanical culture, it seems to me that we must work to retain its achieved values." (!!!) Pandora's box is closed.

Crib Notes

Structurally, *The Gutenberg Galaxy* used four stages to outline the social evolution of man from tribal society to modern humanity—and then back to tribal society.

Marshall defined tribal societies as oral cultures whose members used emotionally laden speech to communicate. These non-literate societies were politically engaged, emotionally charged, tightly woven together, and unified. They lived in what Marshall called "acoustic space."

This space was eroded by the phonetic alphabet. It stripped speech of its emotional dimension, creating in its Finneganian wake linear, individualistic, Western Man— "Gutenberg Man." Beginning in the sixteenth century, the eye overtook the ear as man's dominant sense organ. The printing press was ultimately responsible for the Industrial Revolution, the middle classes, nationalism, and capitalism, ultimately creating a "mechanical culture."

Electronic media, however, beginning with the telegraph, began to morph society away from its mechanical bent. Marshall believed the electronic media were extensions of the human nervous system, with TV being the most significant because it invokes multiple senses.

The punch line—and what made Marshall a star—was his (in the end all-too-correct) assertion that TV, as well as future technologies, would possess the ability to retribalize man back to his oral and tribal roots.

Having Said All This ...

... *The Gutenberg Galaxy* is possibly one of the most difficult to read yet ultimately rewarding books of the twentieth century. It explains so much, all the while taking the reader on side journeys into charming cul-de-sacs and odd dead ends. Written in a self-described mosaic style, its text is hermetic, terse, and often obtuse and draws from sources such as Yugoslavian epic poetry and modern sculpture. Here's an example of its more impenetrable moments:

> A hole in the ground is not enclosed space because, like a triangle or a tepee, it merely exhibits the lines of force. A square does not exhibit the lines of force but is a translation of such tactile force into visual terms. No such translation occurs before writing. And anyone who takes the trouble to read Emile

Durkheim's *The Division of Labour* can find the reason why.

The gauntlet has been tossed.[23] Are you ready for the *Gutenberg* challenge?

Pop!

Marshall reached his global tier of fame with the help of two San Francisco men connected in media circles, Gerald Feigen and Howard Gossage. In 1965 they held a McLuhan Festival in the offices of Gossage's San Francisco ad agency. Emerging journalism superstar Tom Wolfe was there, and he went on to write a seminal piece on Marshall called "What if He Is Right?" Feigen and Gossage also brought Marshall

---

[23] I've found that learning McLuhan is like learning a new language, and about as many McLuhan scholars out there speak McLuhan as do, say, Frisian or pre-1968 COBOL. It is these McLuhan scholars who propagate, out of what might be called a loving and pure sense of fandom, the technology of Marshall's language for the sake of its cool intelligence. But it has always been the often arcane nature of Marshall's ideas, married to his self-described mosaic writing style, that has scared away so many people who would probably rejoice once they began to click with the material. So, even with all the hoopla of the 1960s and well into the tech 1990s and beyond, there exists little self-apprehended grasp of the man's thinking. Most academics have no idea (and no law says they must), but most will confess to believing there's something about Marshall that is original and new. But getting into Marshall is, for most people, like visiting Antarctica. You have to have time, patience, endurance, means, and stubbornness to do so, and once you're there, you're unsure of just what it is you will find.

to New York and introduced him to magazine and newspaper heavyweights through a series of cocktail parties and meetings. He was in all the magazines. He was the spirit of 1965.

But remember, Marshall was in his mid-fifties at this point. He was too old to be a party monster or a rock star or a prima donna; he was a fuddy-duddy in a glen plaid jacket, who, when speaking with executives who had spent a fortune to strip-mine him for insights, was often described as looking like an absentminded prof grading papers. And while hippies may have flocked to him as a guru figure, Marshall saw them as a manifestation of all that was wrong with the way the world was heading. But of course, his policy of not judging backfired—critics mistakenly thought that because he spent some time with hippies he was tacitly endorsing them.

Because of Marshall's increasing American notoriety (a process that was accelerated when he linked up with well-connected and devout fans in the media world), his speaking fees had escalated by 1964 to a minimum of $500 for a lecture or seminar, and he was making forty out-of-town speeches a year. Given his lustrous new fame, the powers that be at U of T knew they had to act quickly before another school poached him. To their credit, they also realized that they would need a whole new category of faculty. Marshall, who was often paranoid about academic Smurfpolitics, could for once take a breath and accept the fact that his fellow academes, while jealous, acknowledged that he was on to something.

Thus, in 1963 they allowed Marshall to establish the Centre for Culture and Technology. It was first housed in his old office on campus, and its purpose was to investigate the psychic and social consequences of all technologies, as well as to foster dialogue between various U of T faculties. It had a reasonable budget, and it was non-bureaucratic enough that Marshall could run the place with an assistant and a secretary, Margaret Stewart. It taught one graduate course, listed somewhat cryptically as:

C&T 1000Y / 1001F&F
Media and Society / A course considering media as man-made environments. These environments act both as services and disservices, shaping the awareness of users. These active environments have the inclusive character of mythic forms and perform as hidden grounds of all activities. The course trains perception of the nature and effects of these ever-changing structures.

Marshall took the centre seriously and was eager to set up experiments that would scientifically measure human responses to media, largely TV, which he believed caused dyslexia because it partially immobilized central eye muscles.

He also wanted to quantify the pleasure people derived from feeling fabrics of all textures and viewing art in all forms.

From half a century away, it all seems hokey and sad and doomed (though well-intended). It also shows how primitive was people's understanding of the brain and neuroanatomy, as recently as the Nixon administration, and it underscores the time lag between having the dream of measuring the brain and having the ability to do so with PET scans and MRIs.

Marshall worked to raise money for a series of tests he proposed and, through connections, scored a $10,000 grant from IBM, out of the United States. The IBM Sensory Profile Study was performed on a number of IBM staffers to see what their sensory preferences were. The results had no practical application, but someone told Marshall that the tests he'd developed could be worth millions of dollars. He freaked out and entered a battle with IBM over who owned what. Thus ended that vein of sensory studies.

Another area of study for Marshall was the relationship between sound and the type on a page. At what point does print stop being silent and turn into noise? This ultimately led to some wonderful books: *The Medium Is the Massage* (1967) and the less popular but fascinating *Counterblast* (1969).

1964: Lightning Strikes Twice

By far the most well-known work in Marshall's career was the unexpected love child of his NAEB report on how to teach media studies to grade eleven students—a repackaging that became 1964's seminal *Understanding Media: The Extensions of Man.* It came on the heels of *The Gutenberg Galaxy,* and about three minutes before youth, black, gay, feminist, and drug cultures exploded and the world was frantic to explain the noise.

In *Understanding Media,* Marshall elaborates on the sensory manipulation of electronic media. He explains that the ostensible content of all electronic media is insignificant; it is the medium itself that has the greater impact upon society. (Yes, "The medium is the message.") Scientists, though, rejected some of Marshall's experimentally unsupported theories. The European black turtleneck sweater crowd—cultural theorists—felt McLuhan dismissed power relationships intrinsic to, and upheld by, both media and its content.

The book is in two parts. In Part One, Marshall states, "The content of a medium is always another medium." He then discusses the differences between what he calls "hot" and "cool" media. For example, a hot medium is exclusive, while a cool medium is inclusive. Hot media are "highly defined," leaving little information to be filled in by the user.

Radio is a hot medium because it requires minimal partici-
pation. Cool media, like TV, are in contrast "low definition"
and highly participatory because the user must fill in the
blanks. This framework for judging media is complex and
often contradictory. It's frequently viewed as problematic, to
the point where it's simply put up with, as it leads to so
many other interesting ideas.

After this it only gets more elaborate and confusing.

In Part Two, Marshall analyzes various media dominant in
1964: the spoken word, the written word (as in a manu-
script), roads, numbers, clothing, housing, money, clocks,
the artist's print, comics, the printed word (as in typography),
the wheel, the bicycle, the airplane, the photograph, the press
(what we now call the media), cars, ads, games, the telegraph,
the typewriter, the phone, the phonograph, movies, radio,
TV, weapons, and automation (manufacturing).

Understanding Media is much more systematic than *The
Gutenberg Galaxy*, but it is more opaque and requires the
same willingness to have your ideas stretched, threatened, or
enriched.[24] The McLuhanism that resonates most clearly

---

[24] The book you are currently reading is a general biography with limited
space—but a quick visit to the internet can fill in many blanks.
Understanding Media's Wikipedia entry is wonderfully done and can elaborate far more than there is space to do so here.

over time comes from it: the concept of the "global village," the world of today created by electrically linked media, a place where humans retribalize through their freedom to bypass time and space.

Perhaps the most charming moment in the book is where Marshall describes Margaret Mead bringing several copies of the same book to a Pacific island. The natives had seen books before, but always different books, one copy of each. When they saw copies of the same book, their minds blew—a lovely koan-like event where the new and the old fused and made fireworks, not bombs.

Understanding Media: The Extensions of Man (Paperback)
by Marshall McLuhan (Author)
ISBN: 8114675357
McGraw-Hill, 1964
Paperback.
Book Condition: Acceptable.
Bookseller: Avia Media
Wilkes-Barre, PA
Price: US$ 1.00
Quantity: 1   Shipping within USA: $3.00
Gift-wrap available.

Add Book to Shopping Basket?

☒ ☒ ☒ ☒ ☒
5.0 out of 5 stars
13 Reviews
5 stars: (11)
4 stars: (0)
3 stars: (4)
2 stars: (0)
1 star: (1)
See all 16 customer reviews…

A tremendously original and thought-provoking work

This is one of the rare works which seem to explain new realities in a way
which no one else before has grasped. It is the kind of work that gives a
'whole new picture of what is happening'. And if for this alone this work
would be of great value. I am by no means a media expert and cannot really
comment on many of the claims of the work. Its virtues are in calling attention to the new media (mainly television) and understanding how it
changed our perception of the world, and of ourselves.

A remarkable collection of nonsense

I have rarely found so much nonsense compressed between the covers of a book. This is a collection of unwarranted, groundless assertions, irresponsible generalizations and shameless one-upmanship. The success of the book in the 60's is proof of the intellectual despair that marked that decade, attempting to get out of the Vietnam Tragedy through false gurus and other unsubstantiated claims to objectivity. The few pearls are buried under such a mountain of bull that it is not worth the effort to search for them. Mr. McLuhan pretends to know about everything, and shows he knows about nothing, with the possible exception of English literature. And even there, his judgments are rarely valid and most of the time intellectually irresponsible. This is not a serious book. Future generations will look at it and judge our enthusiasm for it as proof of our immaturity. I gave it one star because I could not give it zero.

Supernova

At the age of fifty-three, Marshall's ship had truly come in, four years after Elsie's death. *Understanding Media* sold over 100,000 copies in hardcover. It was required reading for members of the global information class, whether to trash Marshall, to praise him, to bullshit about having read it, or whatever. He was everywhere. He was hip and cool and groovy and far-out. He was a fraud, a monster, a genius, and a hoax. Young people loved him. Talk shows were incomplete without him. He was the centre of a spectacle that would have impressed Elsie, and one can only imagine the reactions of his U of T colleagues when Marshall made the cover of the U.S. edition of *Time* magazine ("Canada's Intellectual Comet") or when they heard of Greek cruises with millionaires and Buckminster Fuller and that he was earning up to $25,000 for corporate speeches and seminars.

It's also interesting to observe the creative responses young people had to Marshall—as well as those of TV producers of the era. When creating visual effects to convey the texture of Marshall's words, producers tended to use quick cuts, strobing lights, and woo-woo sound effects intercut with iconic imagery and coloured lights to achieve a McLuhan "look." Forty years later, their efforts seem like a folk-art premonition of surfing the internet, a premonition expressed through the use of soap bubbles, opaque projectors, Moogs, black lights, and randomly assembled 16mm industrial film footage. Anyone working in front of a computer screen with multiple open windows and several applications running concurrently might well agree.

The mark of our time is its revulsion against imposed patterns.
M.M.

Television brought the brutality of war into the comfort of the living room. Vietnam was lost in the living rooms of America—not on the battlefields of Vietnam.
M.M.

Our "Age of Anxiety" is, in great part, the result of trying to do today's job with yesterday's tools—with yesterday's concepts.
M.M.

Is He for Real?

As Marshall aged, his eccentricities became more common and more pronounced. He had a massive collection of jokes and cartoons and loved sharing them with almost anyone in almost any situation—the sorts of corny things your parents email you that have a half-dozen FWD tags in the header. Marshall began his classes and his paid speeches with jokes and bad puns, partly because punning is a pathology (so he had no choice but to pun) and partly because starting an event this way unsettled the audience. *Who is this guy? Is he for real? Is he on drugs? Oh, good God, these are the worst jokes I've ever heard. That pun was atrocious. This guy is nuts.* And then he'd hit them with a wall of ideas, swamping his audience with "probes," forcing them to challenge their basic assumptions, often alienating them, frequently disturbing them, and always leaving in his wake lots to talk about at the dinner table.

Most anyone who attended or audited his classes or went to any of his speeches will agree that Marshall became random quickly. He was tangential and self-contradictory, and could really piss people off. With his protective oblivious coating, it all bounced off him. He was out to stimulate people into making up their own minds and stimulating their own ideas, using his thinking as a catalyst. If they became wrapped up in a specific, it meant they'd lost sight of the big picture. He almost felt sorry for people who took him the wrong way.

There were underlying biological reasons for the acceleration of Marshall's tics and eccentricities. Throughout the early 1960s he began to, for lack of a better word, *freeze* when in public, either teaching or in social situations. He'd be talking and then he would *stop*. His eyes would go blank, and then after a minute or two he'd continue where he had left off. It was disconcerting and worried those close to him. Medically, there were three potential causes for these freezings: perhaps they were mini strokes, or they may have been petit mal seizures (minor epileptic seizures), or they could have been related to a benign brain tumour the size of a lemon found in his brain later on in the 1960s. With each event, Marshall became a bit more of a prisoner of the wiring and plumbing of his head. Biology is not destiny, but it sure sets some boundaries.

The *Massage* Releases

The years 1967 and 1968 were by far the most frantic, glamorous, bizarre, and exhausting of Marshall's life. In 1967 *The Medium Is the Massage* was published. In the three years since 1964, his signature phrase, "the medium is the message," had become a cliché; by punning on his own cliché, Marshall reclaimed ownership of it. Marshall loved collaborating on projects, and his sole job on *Massage* was to sign off on the layouts and the text and provide the title. The book was (Warhol-like) actually written by a McLuhan enthusiast, a writer named Jerome Agel, and it was art-produced by Quentin Fiore, a master typographer and designer.

It is this book that turns most young people on to McLuhan, offering a step-by-step tutorial through the major investigations Marshall and his centre had made since 1963. The book is the graphic embodiment of the hippie era's optimistic side, and it is a quick read—a perfect McLuhan 101 for anyone sitting on the fence. *The Medium Is the Massage* turned McLuhan from being popular into being pop, and it sold a cliché-but-true million copies.

Bronxville

The biggest news of 1967 was in January, when Marshall was named Albert Schweitzer Professor of the Humanities at New York's leading Catholic college, Fordham University. This one-year commitment came with a grant of $100,000, of which $60,000 was to cover the costs of personnel and facilities. It was a dream grant that allowed Marshall the freedom and budget to investigate anything he chose. Oddly, Marshall wasn't at first inclined to accept. He may have been flying off forty or fifty times a year, but that was merely travel. Marshall was a homebody and didn't fancy the idea of being away from his home and family for a year. But, as most of his family would be coming with him, and as he could hire old pals Ted Carpenter and Harley Parker with his research budget, along with his son Eric, Marshall went along with this once-in-a-lifetime gig.

The family arrived in New York in early September 1967 to a huge house in Bronxville, and on September 18 Marshall gave his first lecture to two hundred or so staff and students. Its topic was that war is a form of education, that it teaches people the extent to which media inventions have altered our world and our perception of our own identities. As it wove between the sensibly bold and the offbeat, the wacky and the blatantly offensive, it also discussed the notion that TVs are, in some ways, X-ray machines, and that the speed of communication has turned the world into a global village. In addition, he discussed his theory that changes in communication media were producing a new, invisible environment that was having a profound effect on the world. He made the amazing point that "People aren't that fond of education. So war has been misclassified. It is actually a teaching machine." A few minutes later, he went on to say, "The Negro is turned on by electricity. The old literacy never turned him on because it rejected and degraded the Negro, but electricity turns him on and accepts him totally as an integral human being."[25]

A Gross Insult to the Brain

Students emerged from Marshall's lecture with thousands of little question marks dancing above their heads. This was a dance that would continue throughout the autumn as Marshall's behaviour became odder and odder while a tumour grew in his brain. One evening, at a museum gala, he gave a speech in which he blamed fire trucks for creating ghettoes. (Exactly.) His blackouts became alarmingly frequent, but Marshall never wanted to give any indication of weakness, however slight. Finally, in the fall of 1967, Corinne and the family broke through Marshall's fortress of denial and begged him to get help. He went in for brain surgery on the morning of November 25, 1967. The doctor exercised supreme caution, and Marshall's surgery became, at that point, the longest recorded neurological surgery in medical history.

---

[25] And we're right back to footnote 13.

Corinne and the family had braced themselves for all possible worst-case scenarios (paralysis, profound memory loss, retardation—a terrifyingly long list of possibilities). When Marshall woke up an hour after surgery, the surgeon asked him how he felt, and he replied that it would depend on one's definition of "feeling." He was back again—*phew!*—but he was back in reduced form. He had, in fact, lost swaths of memory; curiously, he had trouble remembering books he'd read many times over. He lived with staggering pain for months afterwards, and he lost some of his ability to be civil to colleagues and students. In addition, his hypersensitivity to noises, always high, became extreme.

The user is the content.
M.M.

The problem in the new politics is to find the right image. Image hunting is the new thing, and policies no longer matter because whether your electric light is provided by Republicans or Democrats is rather unimportant compared to the service of light and power and all the other kinds of services that go with our cities. Service environment's the thing in place of political parties.
M.M.

Distant Early Warnings

Marshall's highly intrusive brain surgery at the age of fifty-six signalled the beginning of an end—the end of the high-water mark of Marshall's fame, his notoriety, his earning potential, his vitality, and his ability to soak up information and to locate patterns. After several months of recuperation time, he was the same man he was before, but things were different, and not merely in his body. The McLuhan Moment was passing, though it would take years for the present to become evident. The daisies, flute music, and love-ins of the 1960s had been overshadowed by Vietnam, Charles Manson, and the Robert Kennedy assassination. The world grew frightened and cynical and cold almost overnight.

The number of Marshall's speaking engagements slowed down. Gary Wolf, an American writer who once wrote a *Wired* magazine cover story posing as Marshall McLuhan's ghost being interviewed online, later summed up Marshall's self-commercialization:

> McLuhan's strange scholarship and unprofitable business advice set him apart from such popular lecturers as Alvin Toffler, Peter Drucker, and even John Naisbitt, with whom he collaborated. McLuhan was stunningly oblivious to the question of how business executives would implement his suggestions and what results would be achieved. His presentations wandered

far from their announced topics, and his audiences often ended up as baffled as his readers.

Trudeau, War, and Peace

In the early 1960s Pierre Trudeau was emerging as the face of Canada's progress and its future. Marshall, like most people, enjoyed meeting celebrities, and Pierre Trudeau was his favourite—a fellow devout Catholic and a man open to new ideas and new ways of viewing the world. Their two-way man-crush expressed itself largely through letters. Marshall was always hoping his discoveries could be used to Trudeau's advantage, and he often pitched ideas, to which Trudeau listened closely. But the thing about Marshall's ideas is that they had no immediate political application. Politicians hoping to gain a short-term advantage through Marshall's books would come away with no new strategies.[26] Not only was Marshall politically neutral in public, but his

---

[26]A Canadian government website (of all places) actually trashes the apolitical dimension of Marshall's work: "McLuhan's conception of the global village has failed to account for the power dynamics in a globalized media environment. Despite recognizing that media had the potential to dominate indigenous cultures, his valorization of oral culture is often Orientalist and romantic. Further, he does not elucidate key political and economic questions, such as global divisions of labor and the widening gap between rich and poor, or issues of capital flow, the environment, migration and national sovereignty as impacted by transnational corporations." (www.collectionscanada.gc.ca/innis-mcluhan/030003-2060-e.html)

work was intrinsically apolitical, in a short-term sense. The only people who stood to gain from it seemed to be the advertisers and media people who came to him (usually cheerfully, and with big cheques in hand, which only further incensed academics). There he was, having devised a genuinely new way of framing an individual's world view, and yet there was no visible revolution, Marxist, industrial, Freudian, or otherwise.

In other ways, Marshall's writing was profoundly political, but its issue was that the changes he (one can't say "predicted") *foretold* weren't overnight phenomena. They were about changes in cognition—cultural shifts that would cause shifts in the evolution of humankind—that would take decades or hundreds or thousands of years to complete. In the relatively short term, much of what he discussed certainly presaged such events as the collapse of communism and the jihad.

On the issue of the global village, rather than being a cheerleader, Marshall was quite the opposite: "When people get close to each other, they get more and more savage, impatient with each other ... the global village is a place of very arduous interfaces and abrasive situations." Also, "All forms of violence are quests for identity ... the literate man is a sucker for propaganda ... you can't propagandize a native. You can sell him trinkets, but you can't sell him ideas."

Perhaps recognizing the absence of an overt political dimension to his work, Marshall co-produced a 1968 book with his *Massage* team, graphic designer Quentin Fiore and writer Jerome Agel. Called *War and Peace in the Global Village*, the book is a collage of images and text that illustrates the effects of electronic media and new technologies on man. Working with a rather complicated idea of human evolution that owes much to Joyce's favourite eighteenth-century Italian philosopher, Giambattista Vico, the book is also an exploration of what Marshall thought to be the ten stages of mankind as evidenced by the dense thickets of *Finnegans Wake*, stages that Joyce called "thunders."

The selection of ten stages is debatably more theoretical than indexical—Joyce scholars take decades to mature, and even then, there's disagreement—but sticking to ten stages did give Marshall a set of parameters to keep him from straying too far off topic.

The fact is that Marshall *did* foresee a long, painful process in which technology shifts would trigger massive identity collapses around the world, which would generate new and terrifying sources of disassociation between the reality of what was physically available to individuals and the unreality of a world depicted by electronic media. The result would be conflict, violence, and war.

But Marshall's visions were more artistic than they were do-it-yourself. They came with assurances, but not with dates or numbers attached. To scan Marshall's books for inklings of what will happen, say, next year, is a poetic or artistic experience—you get a *sense* of the future rather than a prescription or a prediction. One certainly wishes people would give Marshall a fraction of the time they give to dimwits like Nostradamus who actually claimed to see the future. Call it religion or call it optimism, but hope, for Marshall, lay in the fact that humans are social creatures first, and that our ability to express intelligence and build civilizations stems from our inherent social needs as individuals.

Two Navajo Indians were having a chat across an Arizona valley by smoke signals. Midway through their chat, the Atomic Energy Commission released an atomic charge, and when the big mushroom cloud cleared away, one of the Indians sent up a smoke signal to the other, saying, "Gee, I wish I'd said that."

a joke enjoyed by M.M

Q: Why is television not a medium?
A: Because it's rarely well done.
a joke M.M. would have enjoyed

Driving directions to 3 Wychwood Park, Toronto, ON

Start on WELLS HILL AVE, TORONTO going toward NINA ST
go 0.2 km

Turn Left on NINA ST
go 0.2 km

Turn Right on BATHURST ST

Turn Left on ALCINA AVE
go 0.4 km

Turn Left on WYCHWOOD AVE

Continue on WYCHWOOD PK
go 0.3 km

Bear Right on WYCHWOOD PK

Arrive at 3 WYCHWOOD PARK, TORONTO, on the Left

I think of art, at its most significant, as a DEW Line, a Distant Early Warning system that can always be relied on to tell the old culture what is beginning to happen to it.

M.M.

The DEW Line

Marshall and family returned from New York to Toronto in 1968. The big immediate change they made was to move from Wells Hill Avenue to a new address beside Toronto's stately Wychwood Park. The house was upper middle class bordering on ruling class, and was Marshall's last home. Its quiet location lent itself to walking and thinking.

The Centre for Culture and Technology moved, too, into a slightly larger space in a coach house down the road from its previous space. It was messy and cluttered and quickly became beloved. It was another tree fort for Marshall, one containing his secretary, Margaret Stewart, his friend Harley Parker, his brother, Maurice, and his son Eric, although the new vibe was more fractious than in the past; brain surgery had left Marshall more humble before God but also shorter of temper, more absentminded, and somewhat more inclined to take his inner circle for granted.

The summer of 1968 was also when Marshall, along with son Eric and a New Yorker, Eugene Schwartz (who had formed the Human Development Corporation in order to spread Marshall's word), decided to produce and publish a monthly newsletter called *The Dew-Line*. The Distant Early Warning Line was a system of radar stations in the Canadian Arctic, with additional stations in Alaska, the Faroe Islands, Greenland, and Iceland. Its outposts were designed to detect incoming Soviet bombers during the Cold War and became outmoded when ICBMs became the main nuclear weapons delivery system. The newsletter was actually repurposed McLuhanalia printed on vinyl-bound 8.5-by-11 paper and billed as such: THIS IS AN INVITATION TO JOIN A SELECT GROUP OF BUSINESS, ACADEMIC AND GOVERNMENT LEADERS WHO ARE ABOUT TO RECEIVE WHAT MUST BE THE MOST STAR-TLING NEWSPAPER EVER WRITTEN. A book deal arose from it, but the book collapsed. The newsletter also collapsed after a Bahamian corporate retreat also organized by Eugene Schwartz (featuring talks by McLuhan, Buckminster Fuller, and others) ended up being unprofitable and Marshall went unpaid. This convinced Marshall that he was being short-changed on his share of the profits from all of Schwartz's ventures, and *The Dew-Line*, which had limped along anyway, became history in 1970. It must be said that Marshall was a child of the Depression, and the effects of that cannot be underestimated by younger generations. But he was also trained by Elsie to value both success and its trappings. Thus, he lived with this conflict loop: *Don't spend money and you'll survive* versus *Live poor, then you may as well be poor.*

In 1969 Marshall published a slim book entitled *Counterblast.* It featured neo-futurist Dada typography by Harley Parker, and was one way for Marshall to display his stance on revolutionizing linear literacy. The title is a nod to his pal Wyndham Lewis who in 1914 published a two-issue Dadaist magazine called *Blast,* and it pointedly referred to a second explosion of modernity to come, in which linearity is blown apart. The book, while collectible, came and went. Similarly, a collaborative book project seven years in the making between Marshall and old friend Wilfred Watson went sideways after Marshall had problems with the process of collaborating. It became 1970's *From Cliché to Archetype,* a messy plate of scrambled eggs neither man was entirely satisfied with. Yet, like all of Marshall's projects, it contains much richly plowed soil—especially in enunciating the idea that the movement between high culture and low, pop arts and fine arts, is a two-way street—in which the reader may plant seeds and grow strange new flowers.

From Cliché to Archetype (Mass Market Paperback)
by Marshall & Watson, Wilfred McLuhan (Author) [sic]
Bookseller: bilicansdadsbooks
Orangevale, CA, U.S.A.
Price: US$ 1.00
(C$ 1.23)
Quantity: 1
Shipping within U.S.A.:   US$ 3.99 (C$ 4.89)

Book Description: Book Condition: Good.
A CREASE ON SPINE FROM BEING OPENED OTHERWISE GREAT
Immediate shipping.

Bookseller Inventory # 684144

Add Book to Shopping Basket?

Counterblast[27]

McLUHAN, Marshall
ISBN: 0156226707 / 0-15-622670-7)
Bookseller: Textbook Recycle
(Sherbrooke, QC)
Bookseller Rating: 5-star rating
Price: US$ 65.00
Quantity: 1

Book Description: Hurtubise /HMH, 1972. Couverture Soule. Book Condition: Bon Etta + Gilles Robert & Asocial (adaptation De La Marquette Original De Harley Parker) (illustrator). 1 ère Édition Française. 13 x 20.3 Cm. Couverture originale de l'éditeur, propre et illustrée en couleurs. Intérieur sans marque et sans soulignement avec petites taches sur quelques pages. TEXTE EN FRANCAIS. Traduction de Jean Paré. "Le bon sens nous dit que les média sont plats comme la terre". Voilà, en "mcluhanien", tout *Counterblast*, un abc du mcluhanisme, l'oeuvre la plus irritante, mais aussi la plus significative de l'auteur; jeux de mots, jeu de lettres, une remise en question des postulats gutenbergiens, un happening typographique qui bouscule notre confort visuel et, par le choc, nous donne une conscience nouvelle et créatrice de notre environnement. 141 pages. Livre rare en français. Réflexions. Média. Bookseller Inventory # 002487

Add Book to Shopping Basket?

---

[27] A friend of mine is a Microsoft executive who collects McLuhanalia, and for the purposes of this book he loaned me much of his collection, including his first edition of *Counterblast*. It contained a typewritten note from Beverly Gross, the literary editor of *The Nation* magazine in New York, dated September 26, 1969, asking a member of the U of T faculty if he would consider reviewing *Counterblast*.

> Dear Mr. X, Would you like to review the new McLuhan book, Counterblast, to be published next month? We would like something of about 1,000-1,200 words; if the book seems to you a major statement or if you would like to do something more general about McLuhan through it, the piece could be expanded to an essay-review of greater length (up to 1,800-2,000 words).
> Let us know if you are interested and we'll send you the book.
> Yours truly, Beverly Gross, Literary Editor.

Writer X indeed chose to read the book, and also included with my friend's copy of *Counterblast* were a series of handwritten notes (fountain pen, not ballpoint) on the back pages of two photostatted pages from a 1969 Calgary poetry conference. It's entertaining to read Writer X's notes because he was obviously out to totally trash McLuhan even before reading the book. His first note (before he began reading) is "Now it's Harcourt-Brace. As if everyone wants to get a McLuhan." *Hmmm ... don't like that tone.*

The point of this is that, by the late 1960s, even if people chose to review his books—which was becoming rarer (1971's *Take Today* sank without a trace)—those who *did* review savaged McLuhan with a glee that's a bit frightening.

The Same but ... *Different*

By 1973 it seemed like much was happening and yet wasn't happening at the same time. Marshall's condition was still fragile after his brain surgery. His U of T colleagues, after years of poorly suppressed displeasure, had thrown him under the bus, and he lost much of the intellectual support that had remained within the university. His classes still had students, but curious outsiders dribbled away and hecklers shifted from being fiery to being mean. In his classes, Marshall was as idiosyncratic and talkative as ever, but the days of crackling exploration seemed to be fewer.

All of which makes this period sound depressing and grim, but not necessarily for Marshall. Nobody could maintain the pace of life Marshall had endured in 1967 and 1968. Something had to give, and it did: his brain and his health. At the time, Marshall's early 1970s slowdown probably felt to him as if he was simply taking a breather—and by the 1970s most people were quite happy to have things slow down a bit. Society had change fatigue. The decade of the 1960s had been exhausting. The early 1970s arrived almost as a miniature dark age, pointedly heralded by the 1973 collapse of the Western world's economy. On TV, viewers watched the humiliating end to the disgraceful Vietnam War, ducks covered in oil, oil and gas shortages, rampant inflation, and the winding down of the Apollo program. It was a confusing and conflicted time. Hippies were passé, but punk was unborn. There was decadence and decay in the big cities. Cars grew bigger, uglier, and more toxic. There was no map. There never *is* a map, but in the time between Nixon and Reagan, it was simply more obvious. Universities crawled with baby boom children; universities centralized; classes took place in portables; staff multiplied and became more anonymous to each other.

Marshall had another health scare in 1971. An angiogram revealed that his carotid artery was blocked, but it was during the discovery of this that surgeons discovered his feline blood circulation: his external carotid artery (the artery that supplies blood to the face, scalp, and jaw) had formed huge connecting channels through the left base of his skull and inside his skull. Had it not been for his one-in-a-billion vascularization, Marshall's brain would have been toast long ago. He considered this vascularization to be a miracle. Who's to say it wasn't?

When you start to criticize the times you live in, your time is over.[28]
Karl Lagerfeld

---

[28] Twitter, July 20, 2009.

Discarnate Man: Man Without the Meat

New sorts of ideas obsessed Marshall after 1970. One of them was a biblical apocalypse he believed was plausibly imminent. This apocalyptic thinking evinced his more prosaic belief that something was going terribly wrong with society. Marshall ascribed this to his notion of "discarnate man," whose description bears an uneasy comparison to society's general malaise ten decades after McLuhan's 1911 birth.

Discarnate man is an electronic human disconnected from his body (a process also called *angelism*) who is used to speaking to others on the phone continents away while the TV set colonizes his central nervous system. Discarnate man is happy to be asynchronous, as well as everywhere and nowhere—he is a pattern of information, inhabiting a cyberspace world of images and information patterns.

Discarnate man prefers "a world between fantasy and a dream," where barriers fall between consciousness and the unconscious. It is the dark underbelly of the global village—the total loss of identity. Of these "TV children," Marshall said in the 1970s, "I think they are sinking into a world where satisfactions are pathetically crude and feeble, compared to the ones we took for granted thirty years ago. Their kicks are on a seven- or eight-year-old level." He found TV children aimless, undisciplined, illiterate, and anonymous, navigating life with physical and emotional violence.

In the late 1970s Marshall invoked the Catholic Church's concept of natural law, which understands that human beings consist of body and mind, the physical and the non-physical, and that the two are inextricably linked. Because humans have a conscience, they are capable of discerning the difference between good and evil. To Marshall, discarnate man had no natural law. He saw no morality, and this meant mankind was poised for a great religious era, probably destructive and diabolical.

This new era was also one in which surveillance was total, one in which all metrics were calibrated and analyzed. In the 1960s and 1970s this meant nascent spy satellites, TV ratings, credit card data. These days, it means almost anything. At this point in his life, was Marshall losing it, or was he simply seeing his worst paranoia made real and responding accordingly?

AirTV
Astrolink
DirecTV
EchoStar
Globalstar
Hughes Network Systems
Iridium Satellite LLC
Loral Skynet
Mobile Satellite Ventures
Orbcomm
PanAmSat
Spacenet
SES Americom
Teledesic
TerreStar
WildBlue
XM Satellite Radio
XTAR
France Télécom
Stellat
Télédiffusion de France
Deutsche Telekom
OHB System
Hellas-Sat
SES Astra
New Skies
JCSat
MBC
DoCoMo
Superbird
JSC KazSat
Korea Telecom
MEASAT

SUPARCO
Mabuhay
Arabsat
Singapore Telecommunications
Chunghwa Telecom
Shin Satellite
TONGASAT
Thuraya
YahSat
VINASAT
Telenor
NPO Kosmicheskaya Sviaz
Gazkom
Global Information Systems
Intersputnik
Media Most
Hisdesat
Hispasat
Nordiska Satellitaktiebolaget
Eurasiasat SAM
Turksat
ICO Satellite Management
Inmarsat
Optus
APT Telecomunications
AsiaSat
Chinasat
Sinosat
Agrani
ISRO
PT Datakom
PT Pasifik Satelit Nusantara
PT Telkom

Spoooooooky ...

In the late afternoon of March 24, 2009, the moment I finished inputting the words preceding these, I went online and Google's Gmail suggested the following article to me.

Can the Internet change your brain?
By Nick Heath silicon.com
Posted on ZDNet News: Mar 24, 2009 4:57:27 AM

The relentless bombardment of video, music and information online could permanently alter our brains and trigger neurological disorders, according to an eminent neurologist.

With Western children spending more than six hours per day sat in front of a screen, Baroness Susan Greenfield told the Gartner Identity and Access Management Summit it's no coincidence an increasing number of children are today being treated for attention-deficit hyperactivity disorder.

The brain is susceptible to being reshaped by our experiences, she said, citing a recent study where London cabbies who memorized the streets of the capital displayed significant growth in the hippocampus—an area of the brain connected with memory.

Describing the online world, Greenfield added: "You are living in a child-like world of actions and sensations that do not mean anything other than what you see is what you get.

"Screen thinking is strongly sensational, short in span, has no conceptual framework, no metaphors and favors process over concept."

Greenfield said that relationships forged in the "computer world," through social networks and multiplayer environments such

as Second Life, are "intruding on the full spectrum of human relationships.

"Autistic people are very comfortable in the computer world
because relationships do not depend on the tone of the voice, body
language, or pheromones.

"It is literally what you see is what you get.

"I wonder that given the malleability of the brain, whether this
is responsible for the rise in autism."

Unless action is taken our sense of personal identity will be
replaced by the false identities of social networks or the collective
identities on Wikipedia, or be destroyed altogether by a fixation on
the quick rewards of the Internet, Greenfield said.

The Rise and Fall of Faxes ...

Here's where I, as biographer, leave the footnotes and enter the main body text, right now, as Marshall's centre stops holding, once his thinking pixelates in response to his ever more damaged brain.

In 1986 I was working in a Tokyo magazine office, and I heard a whirring noise across the office. I went to look, and I saw a photocopier-type machine spitting out a hand-drawn map. I asked what it was and was told it was a fax machine. *A fax machine*, I thought, *What a novel idea. I wonder why North America doesn't have them yet?* I did some research, and it turned out that faxes evolved in Japan as a means of sending hand-drawn maps from office to office because Japan doesn't really have addresses per se, only contexts. *Hmmm ... you could send more than merely maps with these things ... you could ship documents!*

Cut to 1988 and 1989, when I was working at a now long-defunct business magazine in Toronto. Fax machines, then familiar in Europe, too, arrived in North America, marking the end of the teletype machine. Their price started at around $1,500 and rose quickly from there. I remember a rep from ad sales coming into our cubicle farm, saying, "Faxes are hot! Can't you guys come up with something cool to do with those things? We need to sell some ads."

So my job was to invent cool fax ideas. I quickly learned that it's not easy to make faxes interesting. In the end, I came up with the Celebrity Fax of the Month. Our first was a lipstick kiss from Canadian supermodel Linda Evangelista floating in the centre of a sheet of Hotel George V stationery from Paris. It was serene, and we ran it full size on a page by itself. The next fax was a photocopy of a hockey puck autographed by a recently signed Soviet NHL recruit. It was sent from the Canadian Embassy in Moscow. Next were photocopies of pizza slices from Wolfgang Puck in Los Angeles. ("Last month we brought you a hockey puck. This month we bring you Wolfgang Puck.")

After a few months, though, we were increasingly desperate for celebrity fax ideas. I'd reached the point where I asked the mayor of Halifax, Nova Scotia, to fax me a letter stating how proud he was to be mayor of "a city whose very name contains the word 'fax', the hottest piece of office technology since the photocopier." The mayor was gracious and sent me the letter. Meanwhile, my desperation for fax-fun content only grew worse. Then I had an idea. On a bleak January 1989 afternoon I took a one-hour subway ride, followed by a bus ride up to a Catholic cemetery north of Toronto. The frozen, snowless earth and trees seemed made of cement; the wind made its traditional Canadian *skree* noise. I was cold. I hadn't bargained for such a cold day. I spoke with the cemetery's manager, who gave me a map, plus instructions on how to reach McLuhan's tombstone. And twenty minutes later I located McLuhan's grave—one among tens of thousands, humbly located in no particularly special nook within the cemetery's grid. The stone, using a computer data font, read:

**THE TRUTH SHALL
MAKE YOU FREE
HERBERT MARSHALL McLUHAN
JULY.21.1911 ~ DECEMBER.31.1980**

I'd brought graphite and paper with me and made several rubbings of the stone, but after only a few minutes, the Canadian winter forced me leave. I returned to the bus stop, rubbings in hand. My idea was to send the graphite rubbing around the world via a chain of fax machines, and it worked. From Toronto I sent Marshall's tombstone fax rubbing over to the International Telecommunication Union in Geneva. They, in turn, faxed it onward to the offices of *The Sydney Morning Herald* in Australia. From there, the increasingly murky fax went to the Japan-America Institute of Management Science in Honolulu (my alma mater), then to the *Utne Reader* offices in Minnesota, and then back to Toronto. The image was still legible, and it had the routing codes of its journey tagged onto the ends of the paper. But why Marshall McLuhan's tombstone? Simply because I thought he'd have got a kick out of it. How wrong I was. I'm sure the man would have hated/loathed/abhorred fax machines as much as anything else that was new.

More germane from the viewpoint of two decades later, the trip to the graveyard involved massive amounts of time and energy. The weather was grim. It was a Canadian day. Canada is a cold country; distances are huge. Communication is hard work, and Canadians have to think harder than most when it comes to communicating. And Canadians, bunkered into cozy homes that fight the cold winds, have to think more about the abstract meaning of communication. So do Americans or Russians or Scandinavians, but on a person-per-acre basis, we're the most spread out and have to work the hardest, and because of our history, we have no overriding core belief system that prescribes our thinking for us. And so if, on a cold Canadian day, somebody throws a snowball at you, the medium is indeed part of the message. The same for smoke signals, chalk marks left by hobos, or phone calls made from an Air Canada flight eight kilometres above Saskatoon. Why should a book or TV screen or a fax of a gravestone rubbing be any different?

A Hole in the World

One must approach the decade up until Marshall's December 31, 1980, death in the spirit of grandeur. Part of being old is that you're no longer young, so what made you different and forward at one point in your life starts to work against you later on. Marshall's big marks and thrusts had been made in the early 1960s. There were smaller ideas that followed, but the big ones were over. Marshall's brain, born weird, had endured multiple traumas for decades: big strokes, small strokes, a massive tumour, fantastically invasive brain surgery, and minor cardiac-related oxygen depletion. The man had to feel tired and confused—not only by the era he lived in (or his response to the era), but by his physical body. Marshall did not exercise or diet. This is a man who, when he landed his first job in Wisconsin, celebrated by buying a steak.

There came a point around 1975 when, had Marshall McLuhan not existed, enough people had emerged to fill in the territory he had covered. This is not to deny his genius. If Einstein had never been born, someone else would have deduced the theory of relativity—maybe a decade or two later, but it would have been discovered.

Even with full faculties, Marshall's life and experience might not have prepared him for evolving secular cultural theories, French theories mostly: Derrida, Foucault, Lacan, Baudrillard—Marshall's theoretical overriders. Society had eclipsed the range of Marshall's being.

But there's a different way of looking at it, through the lens of art. If Marcel Duchamp or Andy Warhol had never been born, the world would be much less rich for it. Without Picasso, a bunch of people might have done some cubey-looking paintings, but there probably wouldn't have been Cubism and its many offspring. There would be a hole in the world. In general, when you are looking at a certain aspects of the world that seem boring, you might ask yourself, *I wonder who it was who never got born?*

Anatomy Lesson ...

A longitudinal fissure separates the human brain into two distinct cerebral hemispheres, connected by the corpus callosum. Pop psychology makes broad and sometimes pseudoscientific generalizations about certain functions (e.g., logic, creativity) being lateral, that is, located in either the right or the left side of the brain. Researchers often criticize popular psychology for this, because the popularized lateralizations are often distributed across both hemispheres.

Brain function lateralization is evident in the phenomena of right- or left-handedness and of right or left ear preference, but a person's preferred hand is not a clear indication of the location of brain function. Although 95% of right-handed people have left-hemisphere dominance for language, only 18.8% of left-handed people have right-hemisphere dominance for language function.

Additionally, 19.8% of the left-handed have bilateral language functions. Even within various language functions (e.g., semantics, syntax, prosody), degree (and even hemisphere) of dominance may differ.

Left, Right, Left, Right ...

Possibly as a result of his own neurological dramas, in the mid- to late 1970s Marshall became interested in brain hemisphere theory—lateralization of brain function—in short, left brain versus right brain.

LEFT = VISUAL

RIGHT = ACOUSTIC

LEFT = SPACE

RIGHT = SEQUENCES

Hemisphere theory was fresh in the 1970s, a moment in the history of neuroanatomical studies when brain scientists crawled out of the water, onto land, and managed to breathe and evolve. Lobotomies had only recently been outlawed, but Prozac was still a decade away. New non-invasive ways of studying the brain were emerging that didn't actually involve its being chopped up or liquefied into research smoothies.

Marshall liked the seeming neatness of hemispheric theory. He often consulted on brain science with a Toronto physician named Marcel Kinsbourne, who provided him with what knowledge he could. Kinsbourne noticed Marshall's tendency to hear only those words that were congruent with his theories and little else. Kinsbourne came away from Marshall impressed by his famous protective oblivious coating; he believed Marshall to be one of the most linear people he had ever met—an observation that is congruent with the massive flow of blood into his left (linear) brain.

Every Geek's Dream

Marshall was still pursued by the media during these years, but not exhaustively. His media presence was no longer likened to the spotting of a rare bird. Mass awareness of the effects of media had sunk in, and Marshall's voice had become one of many on the topic.

It was a period of churn. Proposals were made for books that didn't materialize. Business ideas came and went. Marshall and son Eric did a revised version of *Understanding Media*. The years passed.

In early 1976 Marshall agreed to appear as himself in Woody Allen's film *Annie Hall*. It was filmed in New York, and the sequence is the first thing most people mention when the subject of Marshall is raised. In it, Woody Allen and Diane Keaton are standing in a movie lineup, and behind them is a bore blathering on about McLuhan's media theories. What happens is a quintessential geek fantasy, and Marshall did a lovely job with his few lines.

> WOODY ALLEN: You don't know anything about Marshall McLuhan's work.
>
> BORE: Really? Really? I happen to teach a class at Columbia called TV, Media and Culture, so I think that my insights into Mr. McLuhan, well, have a great deal of validity.
>
> WOODY ALLEN: Oh, do you?
>
> BORE: Yeah.
>
> WOODY ALLEN: Oh, that's funny, because I happen to have Mr. McLuhan right here. Come over here for a second?
>
> BORE: Oh.
>
> WOODY ALLEN: Tell him.
>
> MARSHALL McLUHAN: I heard, I heard what you were saying. You know nothing of my work. How you ever got to teach a course on anything is totally amazing.
>
> WOODY ALLEN: Boy, if life were only like this.

Silences

After returning to Toronto, Marshall, now in his late sixties, had another stroke. That fall, he had a severe flu, followed by a heart attack. In 1977 he taught, wrote more articles, travelled a bit, made more book proposals that were stillborn but for one. Editors in general had come to demand that Marshall make his writing less opaque, more linear, but Marshall disliked rewriting. He was swamped by the volume and scope of projects on the go, plus demands to rework them. The one publication that saw light from this era was a textbook, *City as Classroom*, a collaboration with a school-teacher, Kathryn Hutchon, and son Eric. Eric had been nursing the project along since the 1960s, and his determination got the book out the door.

CITY AS CLASSROOM, Understanding Language and Media

McLUHAN, (Marshall, Kathryn Hutchon, Eric McLuhan)
1977
ISBN: 0772550204 / 0-7725-5020-4
Bookseller location: Sioux City, IA
Bookseller Rating: 4-star rating
Price: US$ 86.25
(C$ 106.63)
[Convert Currency]
Quantity: 1   Shipping within Canada:
US$ 10.50 (C$ 12.98)

Book Description: Book Society of Canada, Agincourt, Ontario, 1977. Softcover. First printing. Octavo, orange illustrated card covers. pp (vi), 184, (2). Laid in is the 8 page Teacher's Guide.

A fine copy, no fading, no creases, no owner names. Uncommon nice in first printing, issued as a school text.

Bookseller Inventory # 33286

Add Book to Shopping Basket?

Hardball A Madman
Racial Au Gratin
Mirthful The Milkman
Marital Unloosen
Marginal For Gluten
Martial Muscleman
Morsel The Glue Bun
Harshly Two Slogan
Mortally Prudent
Racial Mohican
Monarchal Cancan
Mothball A Foreman
Minnesotans For Turbans
Misgovern A Sirloin
Vassal Thyroxin
My Sacral Herdsman
Maximal Toucan
Radial Coupon
Harsh The Big Gluten
Monarch An Adman
Marshy My Glue Gun
Lacrimal Toxin
Marginal Woodsman
Madrigal Popgun
Medical Miasma
Moldovan Orphan
Muskmelon Mistral
Muslin Uncommon
Mulligan Oatmeal
Marginal Nobleman
Mortal A Madman
Partial Confusion

When I'm Sixty-five

Marshall had been scheduled for mandatory retirement in 1976 but had been able to get a four-year extension. In 1978, Marshall's secretary, Margaret Stewart, had an accident and was unable to return to work. Her replacement and Marshall didn't see eye to eye on many issues. Tension at the centre increased. In addition, American publishers were sending signals that they wanted their advances back on books that were, after many years, unlikely to ever happen. Money was vanishing. A $26,000 grant came in the nick of time from the Social Sciences and Humanities Research Council of Canada, but the clock was ticking and the centre's future was in doubt.

In the fall of 1979 Marshall arrived to teach his first class of the year and found that only six students had enrolled. On September 26, 1979, he suffered a catastrophic stroke in his office; at the hospital, Corinne was told that Marshall would never leave his bed. It was a Wednesday. Had the ambulance driver turned on his AM radio, he might have heard Blondie's "Heart of Glass," Styx's "Babe," or Dire Straits' "Sultans of Swing." Within six weeks, Iranian militants would storm the U.S. embassy in Tehran and take scores of hostages. Coverage of the 1984 Summer Olympics in L.A. sold to ABC for $225 million. The planet continued rotating.

Marshall's stroke left him unable to read, write, or speak. He could understand conversations but couldn't participate verbally. The arteries that had blessed him had also cursed him. Elsie had died of a stroke, but first it made her speechless, too. Fortunately, Marshall was able to get out of bed, walk around, and participate in the world. And, as happens with stroke victims, some verbal function remained: he could still sing hymns, and he was left with one signature phrase he could use when trying to speak. In his case, it was "Oh boy!" *Oh boy, oh boy, oh boy, oh boy!*—a young Marshall on a Saturday afternoon, sailing a handmade model boat.

Oh, the irony for Marshall. Words—the sound of them, the shape of their letter forms, their intricate relationship to each other, a relationship rendered industrial and homogenized by the printing press—were suddenly nothing but sounds with meaning, prehistoric noises with no means of being recorded or passed forward. They had been stripped of their alphabetical dimension. Marshall had dreamed of a return to a purely acoustic world, and now he had it: it was the worst sort of answered prayer.

Mud And A Boardroom
Pastel Is Sewing
Partly The Showing
Vortical Hoeing
Tactical Losing
Loosening Rowing
Chewing The Young Broom
Carving the Hoosegow
Car Is The Rumor
Arf Goes The Mood Swing
Art Of The Losing
Challenge The Broomsticks
Onyx Reduction
Slam Dance A Big Shot
Announce Five Rubles
Failing The Word Play
The Brain Is Slowing
Words Are Decaying
Meaning Is Draining
Sounds Lose Their Meaning
Noise Overcoming
Photos Sans Soundtrack
Locked In A Nice Room
Hearing Birds Singing
Describe What You Saw
Can't Find A Throat Move
Remove What Once Was
Sounds Like a Big Buzz
Twas Nice To Know You
Got What He Wanted

An enormous part of our mature experience cannot be expressed in words.
Alfred North Whitehead

Speak & Spell

Well-meaning friends and family tried to retrain Marshall to read, but the neural damage was structural and too great. Perhaps a much younger person might have been able to rewire his brain, given time, but not a sixty-eight-year-old man who'd had a massive tumour removed, then suffered a heart attack with accompanying oxygen deprivation to the brain. Devices like flash cards and Speak & Spell toys were tried, but to no avail. In the end, what seemed to make him happiest was to have visitors and friends come to read to him, not unlike his 1961 hospital visits to read Elsie her detective stories.

Word of the stroke quickly spread. It was now 1980, the economy was a mess, and universities were trying to cut what corners they could. With no Marshall, there was no centre. Despite letters from high places, the decision was made and the centre was closed. A trip to its coach house building revealed that it had been vandalized, its files thrown harum-scarum. It brought Marshall to tears.

On the night of December 30, 1980, Marshall had a wonderful evening with friends and family in the Wychwood house living room. The next morning, Michael, the younger son, went upstairs and found his father dead.

One More Story ...

Herewith a second story from *Generation A* inspired by Marshall, in which the collapse of the inner voice—and the sense of self—collides with the eternal plane.

The Short and Brutal Life of the Channel Three News Team

Chloë was sitting at her kitchen table, looking out at the sunny day, when her front doorbell rang. It was the police, come to tell her that her mother had been arrested for murdering the local Channel Three News team—two anchorpeople, the weather guy and four studio technicians. Her mother, acting alone, had arrived at the TV studio carrying an oversize rattan handbag and pretended to be a sweet old thing interested in meeting the hostess from a cooking show. The moment she was close to the newsroom set, she asked to visit the washroom, slipped away, removed several guns from her handbag and came back firing. She was knocked to the ground by a surviving cameraman and her pelvis fractured. She was in hospital, in stable condition. A video of the event was already circling the planet on the Internet. Chloë watched the ninety-second sequence with police officers flanking her; its violence was so otherworldly that Chloë thought she was in a dream. The police asked if she would go to the hospital with them, and she said, "Of course," and off they drove, cherries flashing.

The main entryway was cordoned off, but the cruiser was allowed to slip past the security guards and story-crazed media. They elevatored up to the top floor, where a quartet of officers guarded her mother's room. Chloë had always expected that one day she would visit her mother in the hospital with a broken hip, just not under the current set of circumstances.

"Mom?"

"Hello, dear."

"What the hell were you thinking?"

"I'm more than happy to tell you."

"Wait—where's Dad?"

"He's not available right now."

"Oh Jesus, he's not going to go out and shoot somebody, too, is he?"

"Aren't you quick to jump to conclusions!"

"Mom, you killed seven people."

"Good."

Chloë tried to compose herself while her mother serenely smiled. "So, why'd you do it?" she finally managed to ask.

"Our New Vision church group had an 'enlightenment fasting' up in the mountains last weekend. It was glorious. And during group prayer, I was lifted up above Earth and when I looked down on this planet, it was black like a charcoal briquette. At that moment I realized that Earth is over, and that New Vision will take me to a new planet."

"You're kidding me."

"No, I'm not kidding you, Chloë. Your father and I want you to join us."

"Mom. This is awful. Wake up—wake *up!*"

Chloë's mother looked at her with the same bland face she used when she thanked polite men for holding a door open for her. "You should be thrilled for me, dear. I believe it was *you* who was a fanatic of that comic strip from the 1970s—what was it—the *Yamato*? You of all people must understand what it feels like to want to leave a destroyed planet and roam the universe trying to fight an overwhelming darkness."

"It was just a *comic*, Mom."

"For 'just a comic' it certainly took hold of your imagination. I think you're jealous of me, dear."

"*What?*"

"You're jealous because right now I'm actually inside that cartoon—on the other side of the mirror—and you aren't. But you *can* be. Join us."

"Mom, just stop it. Why did you kill those people?"

"I killed them because they were famous."

"What?"

"The only thing our diseased culture believes in is fame. No other form of eternity exists. Kill the famous and you kill the core of the diseased culture."

"So you killed the Channel Three News team? They're barely famous even here in town."

"If you watch the news right about now, you'll see that New Visioneers around the world have shot and killed many people at all levels of fame. To decide who is 'more famous' than anyone else is to buy into the fame creed. So we have been indiscriminate."

Chloë's sense of dread grew stronger. "Who is Dad going to kill?"

"What time is it?"

Chloë looked at her cellphone's time display. "Almost exactly five o'clock."

"In that case, right about …" Chloë's mother looked at the ceiling for a second, whereupon she heard small cracking sounds coming from the hospital entranceway. "Right about now he's just shot the news reporters covering my shootings."

"Oh God, oh God, oh God …" Chloë ran to the window: pandemonium. She turned to her mother: "Holy fuck! What is wrong with you?"

"Is your father dead?"

"What?" Chloë looked out the window again and saw her father's body sprawled on a berm covered in Kentucky bluegrass. "Yes. Mother of God. He is!"

"Good. He'll be on the other side to greet me with the rest of us who have fulfilled our mission today."

Chloë staggered out into the hallway, gasping, but police and hospital staff paid her little attention as they braced for the next wave of wounded, dying and the dead. She shouted, "Dear God, I am so sorry!" and was ignored.

On a nursing station's TV screen, newscasts were coming in, showing the faces of murdered celebrities from around the world.

Chloë ran back into the room to find her mother glowing.

"Mom, you're crazy. Your cult is crazy."

"I want all of your generation to come join me and band together to smash all the shop windows of every boutique in the country, to set fire to every catwalk, to shoot rockets into Beverly Hills. It will be beautiful—like modern art—and people will finally stop believing in the false future promised by celebrity."

Chloë wanted to vomit. Gurneys loaded with bodies were shunted quickly past the room's door and her mother went on talking: "In the last days of World War Two, the Japanese emperor told the Japanese to sacrifice themselves, to die like smashed jewels. And so I say to you, Chloë, die like a smashed jewel. Destroy, so that we can rebuild."

Outside it had grown dark—not regular darkness, but a chemical darkness that felt linked to profound evil. The moon was full. Chloë and her mother caught each other staring at it at the same time. Her mother said, "I wish the Apollo astronauts had died on the moon."

"*What?*"

"Then it would be one great big tombstone for planet Earth." Her mother popped something into her mouth.

"Mom—what was that?"

"Cyanide, dear. I'm off on your Battleship *Yamato*. Why don't you come, too?"

Chloë ran for help, but the staff were too busy with the wounded, so she watched her mother die, writhing on her bed, then falling still.

Stunned, Chloë walked back out into the hallway. There was blood everywhere. The floor was smeared; the whole place smelled of hot, moist coins. She heard gunshots coming from the elevator bank, and screaming staff ran down the hallway past her. She saw an orderly in turquoise surgical scrubs coming towards her holding a sawed-off shotgun, and the look in his eye told Chloë that this was a New Vision follower.

He was whistling, and as he came nearer, he said, relaxed as can be, "Looks like you're one pretty darn famous little lady now, aren't you?"

Chloë ran into her mother's room and kissed her mother's mouth violently, sucking in the remains of the cyanide. She tasted the chemical as it entered her bloodstream and knew death would be quick.

The whistling stopped as the orderly loomed in the doorway. Chloë said, "Know what? I leave this planet on my own terms, you freak." She was dead before the buckshot pounded her chest.

Meditation 01

Life is cruel. Writing a biography feels cruel. The writer knows when the subject entered the world, what he or she did, and when he or she died. The subject didn't have that same luxury.

What might have felt to a biography's subject like a regular patch of daily life while it was happening turns out to have been a poignant phase of, say, lost options, eroding friendships, dwindling brain capacity, unmet goals, irretrievable lost loves.

M d t t n 01
L f s cr l. Wr t ng b gr ph f ls cr l. Th wr t r kn ws wh n th s bj ct nt r d th w rld, wh t h r sh d d, nd wh n h r sh d d. Th s bj ct d dn't h v th t s m l x ry.

Wh t m ght h v f lt t b gr phy's s bj ct l k r g l r p tch f d ly l f wh l t w s h pp n ng t rns t t h v b n p gn nt ph s f, s y, l st pt ns, r d ng fr ndsh ps, dw ndl ng br n c p c t, nm t g ls, rr tr v bl l st l v s.

e i a io 01
i e i ue . i i a io a y ee ue . e i e o e e u e e e e e o , a e o e i , a e e o e ie . e u e i a e a a e u u .

a i a e e o a io a y u e i e a e u a a o ai yi e i e i a a e i , u ou o a e ee a oi a a e o , a , o o io , e o i ie i , i i ai a a i y, u e oa , i e ie a e o o e .

Meditation 02

Life is grand. Writing a biography is divine. It allows the biographer to retrieve what was seemingly lost or under-valued in a subject's life and whip it back into shape, spritz it with Windex, gild it with gold leaf, and make the world stand up and take notice.

Md tt•☐n 02

L✳f ✳s gr✳nd. Wr✳t✳ng b☐grphy 写作 ✳s d✳van◐. ✳t la▶s th◐ b✳☐grp主题hr t☐ rtr✳v wht ws sm✳世界站ngly l☐st ☐r ndrvld ✳n ✿ sub生命nd j✳ct's l✳f◐ nod wh✳p ✳t bck ✳nt☐ shp◐, sp采取r✳tz ✳t w✳th W✳ndx, g✳ld ✳t w✳th g主题☐ld lf nod k◐ th w☐rld stnd ☐p nod to n☐t低估了一✳c.

~~沉思02~~

~~生命是大。传记写作是神圣的。它允许传记检索似乎是丢失或低估~~ ~~了一个主题的生命和鞭子再次将它形状~~ztirps与xedniW镀金用金箔和使 世界站起来并采取通知

Meditation 03

Marshall always treated people as individuals with souls. He never preached—he may have been an information leaf blower, but he never told anyone to do this or do that. He trusted people to draw their own conclusions, and to have their own ideas triggered by his. Marshall gives comfort and helps us forward; Marshall lets us know that we, humanity, are part of something long and grand, that we're not merely blips on a screen. He has helped us understand the current world and why it's doing what it's doing—and where it may be headed and *why*. With Marshall's prodding, we can choose community over the self, smart versus stupid, reason versus reflex, and, most importantly for Marshall, the soul over all.

Me_dit^{a7ti}on 0E

Mar shall ^{ealwaiys tr_ejat wed} people as in_{tdivid uals} wiltu6h sxouls. Hme neveyr preachqed—hye MWAY HA VE beetn an informa ibtion ^{leaf blo_w}ert, but he neverr torl d _{adny}one to do this oer do _{tsat. He tru} sted people t7o dran w t—h1eir so wn con-nclsu_sikons, and sto have5 their own —deas t_riggecred by his. Mars haqll gives co_mforft and _{hejlps us forwah} rd; Marswhall lets us _{knomqw thcat} we, 3hrum anity, are part of something lon fg hand pgrand, t^{hoba}t we're nuot just ^{blips on} a szcreen. He ahas helped us undgersta_ndd the current worlbd and whyl it's doivng wv hart pit's doihng—annd w_ghere it maay be headed and *wdhy*. 4With Marsh_eall's pro ddigng8, we caon choose comᵖᵐᵘⁿity ocver the self, skmart ᵛᵉʳˢfus stuqpid, rseason2 velrsus reflex, an_d mostb imjp ortantly for Mari9s_h all, the soum l over all.

me _ditza7 ti&n >030 Mar sh all ealwaids tr_____ejat wed per as in_tdivid u als wilt$u6h sxou less. Hme >nev@eknomqw tyr prea____chqed—hyt5his ᵒᵉ ᴹᵂᴬʸ ᴴᴬ ᵛᴱ ᴮᴱᴱᵀᴺ an >inform#lea f-b lo_wert____—but he nDe verr> torl d to do t5his oer do

ᵗsat—he tru sted ttt t7o dran w t—h1eir so wn con-ncls_____u_sikon s and sto have5 his kown ideas t _rigger id eas__ in foot>_HZERS%ARS HAQLL GIVES CO_ MFORFT ____AND HEJLPS U___S FORWAH LETS US KNOMQW THCAT WE, 3HRUM ANITY, A44RE PART >of so loing knomqw talon fg hAND pgrand, thobat we're nuot j$ust blips ____. He ahas helped us undgersta_ndd the current W__ __DRLD whyl it's doivn g wvhe self, skmart ᵛᵉᴿʳˢfus stuqpid, rse&*ason2 vel ruses reflex an_d, ##ly for M ari9s_h all, the souv____vm l ᵒᵛᵉʳ ᵃˡˡ*.

Most of our assumptions have outlived their uselessness.
M.M.

Darkness is to space what silence is to sound, the "interval."
M.M.

So Then, What Happens Next?

To reread Marshall's work as a map for what is to come next for our culture is a tantalizing and iffy proposition. If you had a chill run down your spine reading Marshall's quote from 1962 on page ten of this book, you can rest assured he was right on the money four decades ahead of the biggest shift in human communication since the printing press. With the occasional quick aside, there is little reason to believe Marshall will be wrong in other, smaller things. Will our lives "speed up" even faster than they're already doing? Yes. Will retribalization continue? Yes, but it's not only the big tribes that are coalescing, it's the smaller tribes, too: your neighbourhood Block Watch; Lego collectors; muskrat enthusiasts ... we need not always default to the large and the dreadful. Will theocracies and right-wing leaderships expand? Probably. Even then, there's no saying that new technologies won't subsequently erode those cultures, too, as with the effects of cellphones on Middle East elections. Societies will expand and contract as they always have, but in newer ways, at different rates. Will some new technology devour the internet, making the internet its content? That seems to be likely, and the question is where our collective search for the new might most productively be placed. How *would* one use the entire internet as content—the same way the internet devoured TV and film? Fascinating. Let us reread Marshall with open minds, while remembering that to actively seek out the next technology for its own sake is pretty much a fool's game. If the richest and smartest people on earth can't do it, we can only assume that it will emerge organically from a garage somewhere, the way these things always do.

In any event, I don't think Marshall would be wondering about what technology comes next. His concern would probably be more oriented toward ministering to the human soul and on the way our senses of self and our interior voices cope with ever newer worlds. Marshall's ultimate message might well have been that the body is the medium and trumps all else.

My sense of the current world is that most people assume that other people are inundated and drowning in data, whereas I quite often also note that most people seem to be enjoying, and having fun with, more stories and pictures and words and ideas than anyone could ever have dreamed of. It's not all marketing, persecution, and horror stories—and if the internet did trigger the global financial crisis, we must remember that the world is cyclical. We will return to where we were, but of course *where we were* will be utterly different.

All of us crave drama in our lives. All of us crave meaning, and all of us need to feel needed. Never before have the options to sate these requirements been so plentiful, and never before has pretty much everyone been so aware of the repercussions of stupid ideas or indulgent behaviour. We must find solace, as Marshall did, in natural law—and we must hope that, regardless of the system used to measure human goodness and evil, goodness will always be larger than badness by just one increment.

Exodus

Marshall's life shows us the majesty of the human brain in all its flaws and kinks and wonders. It also tells us about a certain window in time, now long closed, when rules were being rewritten, when nation-states were defining themselves, and the future existed as clearly and wonderfully as a place one might someday hope to visit, like Rome or New Zealand. We can be sentimental about that period in time, or we can move forward, taking with us the best of what was. And part of the best undeniably remains.

As I said earlier, had Marshall not been born, there would have been a hole in the world. There would have been a hole in the sky; a hole in heaven. We are only better for his having been alive.

I chose, in part, to write this book because Marshall's family so closely mirrors my own. A year ago I read a bit of his biography, and it felt as if I was staring at a genetic and ancestral mirror. I heard his voice on YouTube, and it was the voice of my grandfather, Arthur Lemuel Campbell, born in 1900, died in 1971, the handsomest man in the Canadian Prairies, a concrete salesman who drove from town to hamlet to co-op store day after day in all weathers, thinking of I don't know what—all that space surrounding him? The sky and its meadowlarks? The Chevrolet making a new noise; time to take her into the shop? Maybe he was feeling modern as he drove a low-cost gasoline-powered vehicle across hundred-mile grids of mud and rocks and stubble and insect clouds and dumb cattle and wind-bleached barns, driving into the flatness, meeting the people of the Prairies—the English, the Irish, the Scots, the Ukrainians, the Icelanders, the Norwegians, and the Mennonites in Old World garb—thinking of God, thinking of damnation, thinking about polio and socialized medicine and Neapolitan ice cream, and scrimping, and always wondering whether the evangelists were telling the truth or lying or perhaps doing both but not realizing it. A cut from a rusty nail would kill. Pride would destroy your soul. Grain ungleaned was a mark against your soul—your soul! Always your *soul!*

Maybe there'd be a drink for you at the end of the day, a pint, a mickey. Maybe yet another rented room run by an abandoned wife or a bitter scold or a small-minded small-town bitch. Other rooms filled with other men roaming a flatscape only recently wired with electricity and now braising in radio waves. What thoughts would fill the mind of Arthur Lemuel Campbell? Did he hate the past? Did he want to drive into the future, and if so, where did he perceive the future as being—to the west? To the east? Above his head? All that driving and all that flatness, all those Sundays and rooming house meals with pursed lips and ham hock dinners with creamed corn and the fear of God. Our Father, who art in heaven. And always the family left behind—High River; Regina; Edmonton; Swift Current—family gone crazy, family gone religious, family dying young. Don't complain and don't explain. Cut your losses. Cut your family before they cut you. Be weak. Be crazy. Be insane. Be humble. Bow before God. Pretend you're something you're not. Rise above your station and pay the price. Keep your opinions to yourself. Die alone, even when surrounded by others. You will be judged. There will never be peace. There will never be sanctuary, because there will always be something lurking on the other side of the horizon that will be a threat to you. Pay cash. Credit is the devil. This is the year of our Lord, 1930. This is the year of our Lord, 1931. This is 1932. 1933. The sky is cornflower blue, and the clouds are from Hollywood. There's not enough to eat, only enough to get by on. Drive, Arthur, *drive*—there is a future ahead of you. You will live in Winnipeg. You will have children. They will have children. Those children will cut the tether between earth and heaven—or will they? Is there something about this horizontal land that will always bind us to God? What will these monster children keep, and what will they throw away? Technology creates generations: will they be poisoners or will they be merely poisoned? Because this is all somewhere in your head, Arthur Lemuel Campbell, it is and you *know* it, even though you don't know the words, because it is all knit into the land and you are a product of the land and so it is knit into you. It is the twentieth century, and you are driving an automobile through the centre of a continent. The twentieth century will end, and eternity will continue on from there, but you'll be gone by then. You'll never know what came next—the next waves of mutts, the children of the mutts, who somehow became immune to God, robot-ized collective minds that exist everywhere and nowhere. Metaminds with inexplicable biases and wants and unslake-able thirsts—real-time fear all the time—all of which will transpire beneath a sky that will, scientifically, measurably, and indisputably, remain as vast and as flat and perhaps even as blue as it is now, until our sun goes supernova and God conquers all.

Marshall, these were your prairies; this was your land. You craved certain things, and you sometimes got what you wanted. You were in the right place at the right time, and it wasn't random. How do any of us end up being fascinated by some things and not by others? And why do so few of us do the things we like doing? It was an adventure, Marshall, and wasn't it grand? You would have hated the way things turned out, sir, but you would also have found it oh so very, very *interesting*.

Oh boy, oh boy, oh boy.[29]

---

[29] March 2009. Twenty years after I shipped a fax of Marshall's bronze grave marker rubbing around the world via a fuzzed-out chain of faxes, my emailbox received a full-colour, high-res photo of Marshall's recently refurbished gravestone, sent from a McLuhan family member in Toronto. Corinne McLuhan had died in 2008, and Marshall's stone had been cleaned up to match hers. The photo took a fraction of a second to download and could be enlarged and printed and placed on the side of a bus with full clarity.

NOTES

p. 8   *"The name of a man"* Marshall McLuhan (hereafter referred to as M.M.), *Understanding Media: The Extensions of Man* (New York: McGraw-Hill, 1964).

p. 10   *"The next medium, whatever it is"* M.M., *The Gutenberg Galaxy: The Making of Typographic Man* (Toronto: University of Toronto Press, 1962).

p. 13   *"In 1989 a terrific biography"* Philip Marchand, *Marshall McLuhan: The Medium and the Messenger: A Biography* (Toronto: Random House of Canada, 1989).

p. 13   *"an equally terrific biography"* W. Terrence Gordon, *Marshall McLuhan: Escape into Understanding: A Biography* (Berkeley: Gingko Press, 1997).

p. 16   *"To bring order"* M.M., in G.E. Stearns, ed., *McLuhan: Hot & Cool* (New York: Dial Press, 1967), p. 115.

p. 16   *"Instead of tending towards"* M.M., *The Gutenberg Galaxy.*

p. 18   *"Environments are invisible"* M.M. and Quentin
Fiore, produced by Jerome Agel, *The Medium Is the
Massage: An Inventory of Effects* (New York: Bantam
Books/Random House, 1967).

p. 23   *"For tribal man space itself"* M.M., *The Mechanical
Bride: Folklore of Industrial Man* (New York:
Vanguard Press, 1951).

p. 57   *"no derivation and no tendency"* M.M., M.A. thesis:
George Meredith as a Poet and Dramatic Parodist,
1934.

p. 66   *"If he had a weakness"* Marchand, *Marshall
McLuhan.*

p. 68   *"The test is not a means"* This text is from *Wired*
magazine, December 2001.

p. 72   *"In America, low, middle and high are consumer ratings"* M.M., *The Mechanical Bride.*

p. 72   *"Perhaps the world"* M.M., in Gordon, *Marshall
McLuhan.*

p. 83   *"The Trivium"* Condensed from Wikipedia.

p. 87   *"A point of view"* M.M., *The Gutenberg Galaxy.*

p. 87   *"An administrator in a bureaucratic world"* M.M.,
Letters of Marshall McLuhan, edited by Corinne

McLuhan, Matie Molinaro, and William Toye
(Toronto: Oxford University Press, 1987), p. 227.

p. 87 *"Art is anything"* M.M., *The Medium Is the Massage.*

p. 96 *"Canada is the only country"* M.M., in W. Lambert
Gardiner, *A History of Media* (Victoria, B.C.:
Trafford Publishing, 2002), p. 80.

p. 96 *"I don't necessarily agree"* M.M., in Harry H. Crosby
and George R. Bond, *The McLuhan Explosion: A
Casebook on Marshall McLuhan and Understanding
Media* (New York: American Book Company,
1968), p. 174.

p. 96 *"Innumerable confusions"* M.M., *The Medium Is the
Massage.*

p. 103 *"For tribal man"* M.M., *The Mechanical Bride.*

p. 104 *"rampant in the age"* Marchand, *Marshall McLuhan,*
p. 66.

p. 107 *"We look at the present"* M.M., *The Medium Is the
Massage.*

p. 107 *"We shape our tools"* M.M., *Understanding Media.*

p. 112 *"Directions to get home"* Mapquest.

p. 133 *"A commercial society"* M.M., *The Mechanical Bride.*

p. 133 *"Ads are the cave art"* M.M., in Gordon, *Marshall McLuhan.*

p. 133 *"Advertising is an environmental striptease"* M.M., "Media Ad-Vice: An Introduction," in Wilson Bryan Key, *Subliminal Seduction: Ad Media's Manipulation of a Not So Innocent America* (Englewood Cliffs: Prentice-Hall, 1973), p. v.

p. 137 *"less flamboyant precursor"* Paul Heyer, *Harold Innis* (Lanham, MD: Rowman & Littlefield Publishers Inc., 2003), p. 61, via Library and Archives Canada, www.collectionscanada.gc.ca.

p. 161 *"The politician will be only too happy"* M.M., in Marchand, *Marshall McLuhan.*

p. 161 *"When our identity is in danger"* M.M. and Quentin Fiore, produced by Jerome Agel, *War and Peace in the Global Village: An Inventory of Some of the Current Spastic Situations That Could Be Eliminated by More Feedforward* (New York: McGraw Hill, 1968).

p. 177 *"The mark of our time"* M.M., *Understanding Media.*

p. 177 *"Television brought the brutality"* M.M., in *The Montreal Gazette,* May 16, 1975.

p. 185 *"McLuhan's strange scholarship"* Gary Wolf, "The Wisdom of Saint Marshall, the Holy Fool," *Wired* magazine, January 1996.

p. 191 *"Driving directions"* Yahoo! Canada Maps.

p. 192 *"I think of art"* M.M., *Understanding Media.*

p. 212 *"Anatomy Lesson"* Condensed from Wikipedia.

p. 234 *"Darkness is to space"* M.M. and Harley Parker, "Toward a Spatial Dialogue" (chapter 16), *Through the Vanishing Point: Space in Poetry and Painting* (New York: Harper and Row, Publishers, 1968).

ACKNOWLEDGMENTS

Thanks: AbeBooks, Amazon, Simon Baron-Cohen, Ian Ferrell, Google, Terrence Gordon, Nick Heath, Michael Levine, MapQuest, Philip Marchand, Eric McLuhan, Nicholas Olsberg, Bruce Powe, John Saul, Sue Sumeraj, Diane Turbide, David Weir, Wikipedia, Wired, Yahoo!, YouTube, Tom Wolfe, ZDlist Inc.

1911   Herbert Marshall McLuhan is born on July 20, in Edmonton, to Herbert and Elsie McLuhan.

1915   The McLuhan family moves to Winnipeg.

1929   In September, Marshall enters a four-year B.A. program in liberal arts at the University of Manitoba.

1932   An important trip across the Atlantic convinces Marshall to return to England for study.

1933   Elsie leaves Herbert, and moves to Toronto.

1936   Marshall receives his second B.A. from Cambridge. Returning to North America, he takes a job as a teaching assistant at the University of Wisconsin, in Madison.

1937   Marshall converts to Catholicism on March 30.

      He is accepted as a full instructor at the Catholic Saint Louis University.

1939   Marshall and Corinne Keller Louis are married, and on September 2 they arrive in England, where Marshall works for a year to complete his doctorate on Thomas Nashe.

1940   Marshall and Corinne return to St. Louis University.

1942   Thomas Eric McLuhan, their first son, is born in January.

1944   Marshall becomes the new head of the English department at Windsor's Assumption College.

1945   Marshall and Corinne's twin daughters, Mary and Teresa, are born.

1946   Marshall starts teaching at St. Michael's, the Catholic college at the University of Toronto.

1947   Their third daughter, Stephanie, is born.

1950   Their fourth daughter, Elizabeth, is born.

1951   *The Mechanical Bride: Folklore of Industrial Man* is published.

1952   Marshall and Corinne's sixth child, Michael, is born.

1956   Elsie suffers a stroke.

1960   Marshall suffers a severe stroke.

1961   Elsie dies in July.

1962   *The Gutenberg Galaxy: The Making of Typographic Man* is published.

1963   Marshall founds the Centre for Culture and Technology, at the University of Toronto.

1964 *Understanding Media: The Extensions of Man* is
published.

1966 Herbert McLuhan dies.

1967 In January, Marshall is named Albert Schweitzer
Professor of the Humanities at New York's leading
Catholic college, Fordham University.

The Medium Is the Massage: An Inventory of Effects is
published.

Marshall successfully undergoes brain surgery for a
tumour on November 25.

1968 *War and Peace in the Global Village* is published.

1969 *Counterblast* is published.

1979 Marshall suffers a catastrophic stroke on
September 26, rendering him virtually speechless.

1980 Marshall McLuhan dies on December 31, at age
sixty-nine.

COLLECT THEM ALL

EXTRAORDINARY
CANADIANS

Why They Mattered Then.
Why They Matter Now.

COLLECT THEM ALL

EXTRAORDINARY
CANADIANS

Why They Mattered Then.
Why They Matter Now.